CHIEF GALL

CHIEF GALL
Sioux War Chief

▼ ▼ ▼

Jane Shumate

Senior Consulting Editor
W. David Baird
Howard A. White Professor of History
Pepperdine University

CHELSEA HOUSE PUBLISHERS

New York   Philadelphia

FRONTISPIECE A courageous warrior and a gifted speaker, Chief Gall fought to defend the traditions of the Teton Sioux for more than 20 years. In this photograph, he wears a buffalo robe, a proud emblem of plains Indian life.

ON THE COVER White admirers regarded Chief Gall as a fierce warrior and "a man of noble presence." This portrait shows the leader as he appeared in his mid-forties.

Chelsea House Publishers
EDITORIAL DIRECTOR Richard Rennert
EXECUTIVE MANAGING EDITOR Karyn Gullen Browne
COPY CHIEF Robin James
PICTURE EDITOR Adrian G. Allen
ART DIRECTOR Robert Mitchell
MANUFACTURING DIRECTOR Gerald Levine
ASSISTANT ART DIRECTOR Joan Ferrigno

North American Indians of Achievement
SENIOR EDITOR Marian W. Taylor

Staff for CHIEF GALL
ASSISTANT EDITOR Margaret Dornfeld
EDITORIAL ASSISTANTS Annie McDonnell, Sydra Mallery
SENIOR DESIGNER Rae Grant
PICTURE RESEARCHER Matthew Dudley
COVER ILLUSTRATOR Michael Hobbs

Printed and bound in Mexico.

First Printing

1 3 5 7 9 8 6 4 2

Library of Congress Cataloging-in-Publication Data

Shumate, Jane, 1961–
Chief Gall: Sioux war chief/Jane Shumate.
    p. cm.—(North American Indians of achievement)
Includes bibliographical references and index.
ISBN 0-7910-1713-3
Gall, ca. 1840–1894—Juvenile literature. 2. Hunkpapa Indians—Biography—Juvenile literature. 3. Hunkpapa Indians—Kings and rulers—Juvenile literature. 4. Hunkpapa Indians—Wars—Juvenile literature. [1. Gall, ca. 1840–1894. 2. Hunkpapa
Indians—Biography. 3. Indians of North America—Biography.] I. Title. II. Series. 94-13645
E99.H795G357 1994   CIP
973'.04975—dc20   AC

CONTENTS

NORTH AMERICAN INDIANS OF ACHIEVEMENT

BLACK HAWK
Sac Rebel

JOSEPH BRANT
Mohawk Chief

BEN NIGHTHORSE CAMPBELL
Cheyenne Chief
and U.S. Senator

COCHISE
Apache Chief

CRAZY HORSE
Sioux War Chief

CHIEF GALL
Sioux War Chief

GERONIMO
Apache Warrior

HIAWATHA
Founder of the
Iroquois Confederacy

CHIEF JOSEPH
Nez Perce Leader

PETER MACDONALD
Former Chairman of
the Navajo Nation

WILMA MANKILLER
Principal Chief of the Cherokees

OSCEOLA
Seminole Rebel

QUANAH PARKER
Comanche Chief

KING PHILIP
Wampanoag Rebel

POCAHONTAS
Powhatan Peacemaker

PONTIAC
Ottawa Rebel

RED CLOUD
Sioux War Chief

WILL ROGERS
Cherokee Entertainer

SITTING BULL
Chief of the Sioux

TECUMSEH
Shawnee Rebel

JIM THORPE
Sac and Fox Athlete

SARAH WINNEMUCCA
Northern Paiute Writer and Diplomat

Other titles in preparation

ON INDIAN LEADERSHIP

by W. David Baird
Howard A. White Professor of History
Pepperdine University

Authoritative utterance is in thy mouth, perception is in thy heart, and thy tongue is the shrine of justice," the ancient Egyptians said of their king. From him, the Egyptians expected authority, discretion, and just behavior. Homer's *Iliad* suggests that the Greeks demanded somewhat different qualities from their leaders: justice and judgment, wisdom and counsel, shrewdness and cunning, valor and action. It is not surprising that different people living at different times should seek different qualities from the individuals they looked to for guidance. By and large, a people's requirements for leadership are determined by two factors: their culture and the unique circumstances of the time and place in which they live.

Before the late 15th century, when non-Indians first journeyed to what is now North America, most Indian tribes were not ruled by a single person. Instead, there were village chiefs, clan headmen, peace chiefs, war chiefs, and a host of other types of leaders, each with his or her own specific duties. These influential people not only decided political matters but also helped shape their tribe's social, cultural, and religious life. Usually, Indian leaders held their positions because they had won the respect of their peers. Indeed, if a leader's followers at any time decided that he or she was out of step with the will of the people, they felt free to look to someone else for advice and direction.

Thus, the greatest achievers in traditional Indian communities were men and women of extraordinary talent. They were not only skilled at navigating the deadly waters of tribal politics and cultural customs but also able to, directly or indirectly, make a positive and significant difference in the daily life of their followers.

From the beginning of their interaction with Native Americans, non-Indians failed to understand these features of Indian leadership. Early European explorers and settlers merely assumed that Indians had the same relationship with their leaders as non-Indians had with their kings and queens. European monarchs generally inherited their positions and ruled large nations however they chose, often with little regard for the desires or needs of their subjects. As a result, the settlers of Jamestown saw Pocahontas as a "princess" and Pilgrims dubbed Wampanoag leader Metacom "King Philip," envisioning them in roles very different from those in which their own people placed them.

As more and more non-Indians flocked to North America, the nature of Indian leadership gradually began to change. Influential Indians no longer had to take on the often considerable burden of pleasing only their own people; they also had to develop a strategy of dealing with the non-Indian newcomers. In a rapidly changing world, new types of Indian role models with new ideas and talents continually emerged. Some were warriors; others were peacemakers. Some held political positions within their tribes; others were writers, artists, religious prophets, or athletes. Although the demands of Indian leadership altered from generation to generation, several factors that determined which Indian people became prominent in the centuries after first contact remained the same.

Certain personal characteristics distinguished these Indians of achievement. They were intelligent, imaginative, practical, daring, shrewd, uncompromising, ruthless, and logical. They were constant in friendships, unrelenting in hatreds, affectionate with their relatives, and respectful to their God or gods. Of course, no single Native American leader embodied all these qualities, nor these qualities only. But it was these characteristics that allowed them to succeed.

The special skills and talents that certain Indians possessed also brought them to positions of importance. The life of Hiawatha, the legendary founder of the powerful Iroquois Confederacy, displays the value that oratorical ability had for many Indians in power.

INTRODUCTION

The biography of Cochise, the 19th-century Apache chief, illustrates that leadership often required keen diplomatic skills not only in transactions among tribespeople but also in hardheaded negotiations with non-Indians. For others, such as Mohawk Joseph Brant and Navajo Peter MacDonald, a non-Indian education proved advantageous in their dealings with other peoples.

Sudden changes in circumstance were another crucial factor in determining who became influential in Indian communities. King Philip in the 1670s and Geronimo in the 1880s both came to power when their people were searching for someone to lead them into battle against white frontiersmen who had forced upon them a long series of indignities. Seeing the rising discontent of Indians of many tribes in the 1810s, Tecumseh and his brother, the Shawnee prophet Tenskwatawa, proclaimed a message of cultural revitalization that appealed to thousands. Other Indian achievers recognized cooperation with non-Indians as the most advantageous path during their lifetime. Sarah Winnemucca in the late 19th century bridged the gap of understanding between her people and their non-Indian neighbors through the publication of her autobiography *Life Among the Piutes*. Olympian Jim Thorpe in the early 20th century championed the assimilationist policies of the U.S. government and, with his own successes, demonstrated the accomplishments Indians could make in the non-Indian world. And Wilma Mankiller, principal chief of the Cherokees, continues to fight successfully for the rights of her people through the courts and through negotiation with federal officials.

Leadership among Native Americans, just as among all other peoples, can be understood only in the context of culture and history. But the centuries that Indians have had to cope with invasions of foreigners in their homelands have brought unique hardships and obstacles to the Native American individuals who most influenced and inspired others. Despite these challenges, there has never been a lack of Indian men and women equal to these tasks. With such strong leaders, it is no wonder that Native Americans remain such a vital part of this nation's cultural landscape.

9

1

"DO YOU WANT THAT BAD SIOUX?"

The Hunkpapa war chief Gall distinguished himself early in life as a skilled hunter and warrior. By the mid-1860s, he had become a central force in the fight to preserve Lakota freedom.

On a cold day in December 1865, a young man named Gall and a small group of followers could be found traveling across the plains in what is now south-central North Dakota. Gall was about 25 years old—a tall man with a broad, powerful build, thoughtful eyes, wide, full lips, and long black hair. December in that part of the country could get as cold as 40 degrees below zero, and Gall and his people wore heavy robes and moccasins of buffalo hide, the warm fur turned inside. Gall belonged to a small Native American tribe called the Hunkpapas, who occupied the grassy plains between the Missouri River and the mouth of the Yellowstone, living off the buffalo that ranged there. The Hunkpapas were a branch of a larger tribe who called themselves the Lakotas, and whom white traders referred to as the Sioux. East of the Missouri River, the tribe had relatives called the Dakotas. Both *Lakota* and *Dakota* were words that meant "friend" or "ally."

Gall was traveling to Fort Berthold, which lay on a broad bluff overlooking the Missouri River where it bends west toward what is now Montana, in order to do business with the white traders there. He and his people probably traveled in a cluster, some on horseback, others walking. Their horses and dogs may have been laden with packs or harnessed to travois—sleighs made of long, slender poles with hides stretched tightly between them. One end of the travois was bound to the animal; the other end trailed far behind on the ground, carrying food, supplies, and hides for trading. The Lakotas had been trading with whites since well before Gall was born, bringing to Fort Berthold and other posts the hides of the buffalo, antelope, and other animals they had hunted in the summer and exchanging them for manufactured goods: firearms, ammunition, knives, pots, and kettles. The Lakotas and

Indian traders approach Fort Berthold, a U.S. post on the Missouri River.

neighboring tribes had permitted traders to set up exchange posts on their land in the early 1800s, and relations between the two were generally friendly.

This was not the case, however, with another group of whites that had begun to enter Lakota territory when Gall was a child: emigrants headed for the Far West. Although these people generally traveled straight through Lakota territory without claiming any of the Indians' land, their long wagon trains frightened away the buffalo, which the plains tribes depended on for their livelihood. The buffalo were crucial to every aspect of Lakota life. They were the Indians' source of food, clothing, shelter, and trade; the Lakotas' yearly buffalo hunts were the heart of their culture. The steady, disruptive stream of emigrants angered the Lakotas, and from time to time they would try to interrupt it by raiding the wagons as they passed.

A few years after the first settlers came through, when Gall was about 10, another group of white people had appeared: U.S. government officials and soldiers. The Lakotas and their neighbors had resented the settlers, but these newcomers alarmed them even more. Although the officials offered to provide the Lakotas with food and goods to make up for the losses in their hunting, these provisions were usually meager, and a life of waiting for inadequate food, rather than ranging the plains and hunting as they always had, did not appeal to many of the Lakotas. They wanted simply to be rid of the settlers and soldiers and to return to their traditional way of life. Meanwhile, whether the Indians accepted their gifts or not, the whites were determined to clear the way for the settlers to pass through Lakota territory.

The officials began protecting the settlers by building forts along their roads. By the mid-1860s, thousands of U.S. soldiers were in Lakota territory, carrying out their

plans despite the Indians' resistance. During the summers of 1864 and 1865, Gall and other Hunkpapas had encountered large companies of soldiers on their hunting grounds and had met these whites in battle.

In some ways these confrontations resembled the battles between the Lakotas and their traditional enemies, the Crows, Arikaras, and Assiniboins. When one group trespassed on the other's territory, both sides expected to fight, and the victors came away with the scalps and horses of their enemies. Yet when the Lakotas fought the whites, they encountered a fighting style very different from that of their Indian opponents, and their usual tactics often failed them. Traditional plains Indian war-

Tracking a buffalo herd, two hunters in snowshoes move in for the kill in an 1833 painting by George Catlin. As settlers and U.S. troops began moving across Lakota territory, they frightened the buffalo and disturbed the hunt, a foundation of plains Indian culture.

fare generally consisted of fast attacks made by small groups of men who were bent on gaining honor through their own acts of daring. The white soldiers were less interested in individual honor than in victory as an organized group, and with their more powerful weapons, they were usually able to overwhelm the Lakotas at the outset. Little by little, the U.S. troops had succeeded in driving the Lakotas away from the immigrant roads.

In the fall of 1865, the Lakotas had retreated to the sheltered valleys of the north and begun making preparations for the cold winter months. One bitter result of the summer's warfare was that in fleeing the whites, the Lakotas had abandoned the buffalo meat and hides they had prepared for the winter, which the soldiers had then destroyed. Now, in December, Gall was lucky to have anything to trade at all, for many of the Lakotas and their neighbors were practically starving. Some, in fact, were so hungry and so afraid of the military that they were prepared to do anything the government wanted. Just two months before, U.S. agents had traveled to Fort Sully—one of the new outposts in Lakota territory—to make a treaty exchanging food for the settlers' safe passage, and they had persuaded many of the Lakotas to sign.

But several prominent Lakotas—including Gall's longtime friend Sitting Bull, and Red Cloud, a chief of the Oglala branch of Lakotas—were becoming more determined and articulate in their resistance. The only white people who had legitimate business in Lakota territory, they thought, were traders; the settlers, soldiers, and officials should leave. If not—if they persisted in building forts and establishing roads when they had been told by important chiefs not to—they would be treated as an enemy tribe. Gall associated with such men as Sitting Bull and Red Cloud and shared many of their views. But

he was younger than they, and that December as he came to trade at Fort Berthold, he may not have been quite so resolved in his opposition to white intrusion.

Certainly he was prepared to meet peace with peace, and in the past, trading had generally been a peaceful occasion. When Gall and his people arrived at the gates of Fort Berthold, the women in the group cleared the ground beneath the willows to make a smooth base for their tipis. These shelters—made of dressed buffalo hides stretched over a framework of poles—were easily transported and reconstructed. As the women set up camp, the men tended the animals. No one scouted the area for enemies, for they were in Hunkpapa territory, and they considered themselves secure.

But in fact they were being carefully watched. Not far away, a young Arikara warrior named Bloody Knife was perched on a scaffold, looking on with great interest. The Hunkpapas and the Arikaras had always been adversaries, but between Gall and this young man there was a special enmity. Although Bloody Knife's mother was an Arikara, she had married a Hunkpapa warrior and settled among the Hunkpapas shortly before Bloody Knife was born. As a boy, Bloody Knife had been unhappy among the Hunkpapas, especially because some of the Sioux boys—including Gall, who was about his own age—had teased and tormented him for belonging to an enemy tribe. When Bloody Knife was about 12, he and his mother had fled the Hunkpapas and returned to the Arikaras. He had visited his father's camp a few times since then, and his resentment toward the Hunkpapas, and particularly toward Gall, had only intensified.

Gall was a powerful warrior who had distinguished himself early in his life for his strength, skill, and courage, and he had never been intimidated by Bloody Knife. Had he known that his rival was following him, however, he

Gall's rival Bloody Knife (left) and a group of U.S. soldiers display a hunting trophy during an 1874 expedition to the Black Hills. In the center of the photograph is Lieutenant George Armstrong Custer, who two years later would lead a fateful campaign against the Sioux.

might have been cautious. For not only did Bloody Knife nurture a grudge against Gall, but he had done things that Gall found unconscionable: he had become a guide for the U.S. soldiers and was living off their food rations. The summer before, Bloody Knife had even assisted government troops as they fought the Hunkpapas.

As soon as Bloody Knife was certain he had found Gall, he ran to Fort Berthold, where General Alfred Sully, a leader in the recent warfare with the Lakotas, had stationed his soldiers. Bloody Knife asked the commanding officer if he wanted "that bad Sioux who has been killing these white men found dead and scalped in lonely places along the river." Immediately, the officer ordered a lieutenant and a platoon of soldiers to follow Bloody Knife to the Sioux encampment.

The soldiers quietly approached the clearing and surrounded Gall's tipi as the Hunkpapas ate and rested inside. The troops waited, poised for action, and eventually Gall emerged from his lodge; before he knew what was happening, a bullet struck him, and he fell to the ground. Then a soldier dashed up and rammed his bayonet through Gall's thick chest, pinning him to the ground. Another soldier quickly followed, stabbing Gall through the neck. As blood streamed from Gall's wounds and mouth, the lieutenant in charge of the attack walked over, bent down to examine the bleeding body, and proclaimed him dead.

Bloody Knife, however, was not satisfied. He too came over to his enemy's prostrate body and shoved his gun near Gall's bloodied face. A split second before he pulled the trigger, the lieutenant—perhaps preferring not to extend the violence—pushed the gun to one side, and its discharge tore up the ground a few inches from Gall's head. Their mission completed, the platoon and a frustrated Bloody Knife returned to the fort, leaving Gall's body bleeding in the snow.

The next morning, however, held a surprise. For when Bloody Knife returned to the spot to scalp the body—a crucial act, by which he could claim coup, or conquest—he found nothing. There was no sign of Gall; Bloody Knife had lost his prize. Bloody Knife later learned that Gall's party had included an elderly woman who was especially skilled in healing, and Gall had been taken to her by one of his wives. After Gall was treated, Bloody Knife believed, the whole group had fled the fort, carrying the injured warrior by travois.

Other versions of his recovery exist, but out of all these accounts, only one fact is certain: Gall survived. Those who knew him believed that it was not just the efficacy of Hunkpapa medicine but also his extraordinary strength and constitution that saved him. Gall, like other young Lakota warriors, had trained his body to endure pain and overcome adversity.

The attack left permanent scars on Gall's body; it left an even deeper impression on his mind. He had long been committed to preventing the whites from taking what belonged to his people, but until he was assaulted at Fort Berthold he had probably believed he could trade with them peacefully. After the assault, however, his determination was strengthened by hatred and contempt, both for the soldiers who would attack an unsuspecting man on a peaceful mission and for the Indian scout who would help them. Gall was now resolved not only to defend the Hunkpapas and their land from the intrusions of settlers, soldiers, and officials, but also to keep his people united against the whites in all their undertakings.

2

BLOOD ON THE PRAIRIE

In this 19th-century engraving, an Indian hunter procures metal tools and weapons—commodities that transformed life for the Lakotas and many other tribes. From the time Europeans first arrived in North America, the fur trade played a pivotal role in relations between whites and Indians.

Gall was born around 1840 on the Moreau River, a branch of the Missouri River in what is now South Dakota. At the time of his birth, the Lakotas had been living in that part of the country for only a century. Previously, they had lived as one tribe with the Dakotas near the head of the Mississippi River, where they had fished, hunted, and gathered wild fruits and vegetables. By the mid-1700s, French traders had become well established in this area, and soon the Ojibwas—longtime enemies of the Dakotas—had begun using their newly bought European weapons to take control of the region. The Ojibwas called the Dakotas *nadoueissiw,* or "snakes," and it is from this word that the French derived the name *Sioux.* Threatened by the Ojibwas, some of the Dakotas moved west around 1740, and they became known as the Teton Sioux, or the Lakotas. They remained allied with their relatives to the east, however, and the eastern and western tribes together became known as the Sioux Confederation. The Lakotas included seven allied subtribes: the Oglalas, Brulés, Minneconjous, Two Kettles, Hunkpapas, Blackfeet, and Sans Arcs. The Hunkpapas, to which Gall belonged, were a small tribe, with only several hundred families, and they often hunted and camped with the Blackfoot and Sans Arc Sioux.

21

On the plains, the Lakotas made two acquisitions that, together with their new environment, transformed their way of life. From French traders they procured firearms, and from the Indians to the southwest they acquired horses, which had been introduced into North America several centuries earlier by Spanish explorers. These new tools allowed the Lakotas to hunt buffalo, the largest and most imposing game in the area. Not long after arriving on the western plains, the Lakotas had fashioned a life that fully exploited their new resources, a life that revolved around hunting, warfare, and rapid movement. The buffalo gave the Lakotas almost everything they needed to survive, for nearly every part of the animal was used: the meat for food, the hide for clothing and shelter, and even the hooves for glue and the dung for

A band of Lakotas celebrates the Sun Dance in a painting by Short Bull, an Oglala war chief.

fuel. Buffalo hides, additionally, could be exchanged with white traders or other tribes for metal utensils, weapons, and corn or other produce. Through warfare the Lakotas extended their domain and enlarged their stock of horses, steadily increasing their wealth and prestige. Warfare also gave young Lakota men a chance to prove their courage and strength. Great success in hunting and in combat could in fact make a young man a chief.

Because the livelihood of the Teton Sioux depended on the land, their life changed with the seasons. Winters on the prairies and plains were so cold, windy, and snowy that the Lakotas generally settled in camps of large family groups, or bands, in sheltered regions such as creek bottoms to wait out the cold season, living on the dried food they had gathered and prepared during the warmer months. But as soon as the snow had melted and the grass had grown long enough to fatten the buffalo, they collected into larger camps for the hunting, warfare, and festivals that went on throughout the summer as they followed the great herds across the plains. When the tribe's men brought home the day's kill, the women prepared the hides and dried the meat, which they mixed with berries to form the tribe's winter staple, called pemmican.

Hunting buffalo required caution and discipline, for any recklessness or sudden action on the part of the hunters might send the herd stampeding. To guard against such mishaps, the Lakotas appointed policemen, or *akicitas*, who marshaled the younger hunters and enforced the will of the tribe's councils, which were made up of the elders and the chiefs of the various small bands. The akicitas were drawn from prestigious secret war societies, to which only the bravest and most talented warriors could belong.

Just as the Lakotas' daily life depended on the land,

so too did their religion. They believed that deities were present everywhere in the world, and that they influenced each part of life; many of these spirits were benevolent, but others were not. The bad spirits were always trying to disrupt life. For example, the Mini Watu—tiny creatures that looked like maggots—rotted food, and if they got inside the human body, they caused sickness and pain. The good spirits, on the other hand, could guide or lend their power to the Lakotas in all aspects of life. Tatanka, for instance, was the buffalo god, who watched over the hunt; Tate, the wind, determined the seasons. The center of Lakota religion, however, was Wakan Tanka, the "Great Mysterious." This spirit was both a being in itself and a combination of the four most powerful benevolent deities: Skan, the sky, who watched over and judged everything; Maka, the earth, who was the source of food, water, material goods, and all things that grew; Inyan, rock, who represented ancestry and authority; and, most important, Wi, the sun, who presided over the four great virtues: bravery, fortitude, generosity, and wisdom.

Worship of Wi provided the single most important religious event in Lakota culture: the Sun Dance. This ceremony took place each summer and involved some eight days of feasting and dancing. It culminated in a ritual in which men attached themselves to a tall central pole by means of leather thongs inserted beneath the skin on their chest. They danced slowly around the pole, sometimes increasing their weight by attaching buffalo skulls to the skin of their backs, staring at the sun, Wi, until the thongs finally pulled through their skin. The ritual gave the dancers a direct, emotional, and self-sacrificing connection with the source of power and virtue—qualities they hoped to gain for themselves and their people.

This engraving by Frederic Remington, a popular artist of the American West, shows young plains Indians breaking a colt. The Lakotas valued horsemanship as highly as they did hunting and fighting skills, and the size of a warrior's pony herd was the main measure of his wealth.

Young Lakota boys began to develop the four virtues of Wi from the very beginning of their training as hunters and warriors. This rigorous training—which taught them how to handle bows and arrows, spears, knives, tomahawks, shields, and muskets; how to master horses, and to ride so close to the enemy they could actually touch him with a "coup stick" and claim a conquest—was usually directed by their fathers, although mothers were responsible for boys' development until they reached puberty.

Gall probably learned his skills from more distant male relatives, for his father died when he was less than a year old. Growing up without a father, he may have missed some of the special guidance that other boys enjoyed, but there is no doubt that he was well taken care of. In Hunkpapa society, boys called all their older male relations "father," and all of these men took an interest in the young boys' welfare. The Lakotas were known for treating their children with great fondness and indulgence; a Lakota tribesman once explained, "a child is the greatest gift from Wakan Tanka."

From the time of a child's birth, Lakota parents eagerly looked for signs of a promising character. Gall's abilities, according to a fellow Sioux named Ohiyesa, became apparent one summer when he was three years old, as the tribe was moving up the Powder River in search of buffalo. At that time he was still known by his childhood name, Matohinshda, or Bear-Shedding-His-Hair. His mother, following a common Lakota practice, had set him in a travois harnessed to a dog and was walking along beside him, digging for roots as she went. Suddenly, a rabbit crossed their path, and the dogs—including the one pulling Matohinshda—bolted after it. Gall rattled behind his runaway dog, gripping its tail in one hand and a travois pole in the other, his hair streaming, until in a last dash the dog caught the rabbit in his jaws. While Gall's mother ran to her boy and clutched him, his grandmother poured some water for the dog, and an older man declared the event an omen: Matohinshda's brave exploits would draw his people's notice once again. Another childhood event, however, warned of a darker future. During a particularly difficult time for the tribe, Matohinshda was found eating the gallbladder of an animal carcass in an effort to appease his hunger. It was with this incident, a portent of the hard days to come, that Gall earned his adult name.

As Gall grew older, he often demonstrated his strength and promise. Ohiyesa, later known as Dr. Charles Eastman, tells of an incident in which the Lakotas met a group of Cheyennes—a tribe with which they had been friendly for many years—at an intertribal gathering. The two tribes held a huge wrestling match, pitting Lakota

A band of Sioux moves from one encampment to another, transporting the tribe's belongings by travois.

boy against Cheyenne boy in a long line. Gall was set against a boy named Roman Nose. The boys began to wrestle, and one by one each pair had a victor, except for Gall and Roman Nose. They remained locked in battle long after the others had finished, until finally Gall laid his opponent sprawling on the ground, and Roman Nose's mother stepped forward to place a beautiful buffalo robe over Gall's shoulders, proclaiming him the champion.

By the time he was a teenager, Gall had so distinguished himself in the tribe's many battles that he had become a member of the most prestigious men's society, the Strong Hearts, and a close friend of the eminent warrior Sitting Bull. Sitting Bull was about nine years older than Gall, and somewhat shorter, with a large head and stocky build. He played the role of older brother to his admiring companion; in a few decades, they would become two of the best known and most feared of all Sioux warriors.

Such strong, skilled, and ambitious young men as Sitting Bull and Gall were the pride of the Lakotas. In the future, it would be their job not only to assure the tribe a plentiful supply of buffalo and horses but also to protect Lakota lands from hostile neighbors, thus preserving their peoples' proud reputation. During Gall's childhood, the Lakotas had enjoyed the most impressive war record of any of the plains tribes, having pushed aside Crows, Omahas, Pawnees, and Poncas in order to rule the land ranged by the buffalo. So confident were they in their strength, in Wakan Tanka, and in an endless supply of buffalo and horses that it probably would have surprised Gall to know that the Lakota "empire" and the life he and his people cherished had already begun to erode.

Only two years after Gall was born, something had happened that threatened to change this life drastically: the first emigrant wagons had rolled west through Lakota territory. In earlier times, an invisible line had been drawn down the middle of North America, along the western borders of what are now Minnesota, Iowa, Missouri, Arkansas, and Louisiana. West of this line were lands that the U.S. government did not consider livable—at least not by white farmers. The United States had dubbed the line the Permanent Indian Frontier and the territory west of it Permanent Indian Country. By the 1840s, however, tales of the fertile valleys of the Far West—in the present-day states of California, Oregon, and Washington—had begun to attract settlers, and to get to those new lands, they had to pass through Permanent Indian Country.

The first emigrants traveling west were bound for Oregon and had no interest in Lakota territory; they simply had to pass through it to get where they were going. But behind them they left wheel ruts, refuse, trampled grass, and sometimes even the shallow graves of people who had died along the way. As more of these emigrants journeyed west, their trail of destruction and debris became more and more noticeable.

For the Lakotas, this intrusion meant above all a disruption of their usual hunting patterns. Wary of the traces left by the settlers and finding wide swaths of their grasslands depleted, the buffalo would not cross the Oregon Trail, as the emigrant road was called, and altered their path to avoid it. With the Oregon Trail dividing their lands, the Lakotas could not track the herds as easily as they once had, and their hunting suffered. Frustrated, they began harrassing the emigrants as they passed along the trail, an act that attracted the attention of the U.S. government.

In 1845, federal officials sent a representative to meet with the Lakotas and assure them that the government wanted only peace; the agent was to back up this message, however, with a show of military power. If the Lakotas had hoped to halt the flow of emigrants, they were disappointed, for more appeared. First the Mormons, headed for Utah, set out on a new path just north of the Lakota hunting grounds along the Platte River; then, in 1849, after gold was discovered in California, thousands of eager miners also began crossing the plains. This torrent of travelers effectively transformed all life on the prairies: the buffalo fled north and south, never again returning to the Platte River region, and the Indians began suffering from both hunger and cholera—a Euro-

A wagon train passes Fort Laramie on the North Platte River, where in 1851 the Lakotas and other plains tribes attended their first treaty council with the U.S. government.

pean disease brought by the emigrants. The Lakotas' raids on the emigrant trails continued.

In 1849, the United States purchased the American Fur Company's trading post on the North Platte River and renamed it Fort Laramie. Two years later, hoping the Indians could be dealt with peaceably, the Commission of Indian Affairs arranged for a grand council of plains tribes to meet at this new government post. Attending the council were as many as 12,000 Native Americans, including representatives from the Lakotas and some of their traditional enemies.

According to the treaty introduced at Fort Laramie, Indians were to let the emigrants pass through their country in peace. The tribes were also asked to stop warring among themselves, as their fighting affected the welfare of the settlers. In return, the government promised to pay for the losses the Indians suffered as a result of the traffic through their land and to provide the tribes with an annual supply of food and farming goods for 50 years.

As reasonable as this treaty may have sounded to the commission, it was doomed to fail. Several tribes, including the Hunkpapas, never signed the document, and few of those who did sign it understood it. Aimed at ending intertribal hostilities, the treaty divided the plains into territories, but the borders it drew were often very different from those recognized by the tribes themselves. And no tribe had any intention of ending traditional warfare against its enemies; for most plains tribes, fighting had become a way of life. Essentially, the treaty had been drafted by one culture for another, with very little understanding of the differences that existed between them.

After the council at Fort Laramie, rifts began to develop between those who were willing to accept the annuities offered by the United States and those who were not. Many Indians regarded accepting the rations as a first step toward capitulation. This faction believed that the people depending upon the government's supplies would soon abandon all their old ways and live as the government wanted. Gall was only a boy when this first treaty with the United States was signed, but the issues it presented were to preoccupy him for most of his life.

The weakness of the Fort Laramie treaty became apparent in 1854, when tensions between Indians and U.S. officials reached the breaking point. That summer, as a group of Mormons passed along the road near Fort Laramie, one of their oxen strayed from the trail, and a hungry young Minneconjou warrior, who was camped near the fort with a party of Brulés, shot the animal. Although the young man was willing to pay for his kill—all that the Laramie treaty required of him—the Mormon owner was unsatisfied. When Lieutenant Grattan, a brash young officer stationed at Fort Laramie, intervened, the situation exploded in a battle that left the Brulé chief and 30 soldiers dead. After this incident, which marked the first bloodshed of U.S. troops on the plains, the government decided it would "discipline" the Lakotas.

In the summer of 1855, Colonel William Harney arrived in Lakota territory with more than 1,000 men. Determined to gain the Lakotas' respect through terror, he attacked one of their camps just off the Platte River. Harney and his men killed nearly 90 people, including many women and children. He then called the Lakotas to a council at Fort Pierre, some 250 miles northeast of Fort Laramie, where he dictated a new treaty. Harney's council was as unrealistic as its predecessor five years before, and his treaty never became law. The episode nevertheless affected the Lakotas, for after Harney's "rub-out," as the 1855 massacre was termed, many Indians were convinced that the U.S. government would, one way or another, get what it wanted from them. At this point, in fact, the United States, whose territory stretched across the continent, was well on its way to vanquishing the plains tribes so that its domain would be unbroken.

By this time Gall was in his late teens, and he had already begun to demonstrate the strength, skill, and daring that would make him a formidable leader. By the late 1850s, Gall, Sitting Bull, and several other prominent warriors had founded the Midnight Strong Heart Society, an elite secret group within the Strong Hearts that gathered for late-night ceremonies and, according to some accounts, instructed its members to wear special costumes when they rode into battle. At about this time, Bloody Knife and his mother fled the Hunkpapas—many of whom, including Gall, had made them unwelcome—and returned to her native Arikaras.

In 1857, deeply troubled by their relations with the U.S. government, the Lakotas decided to hold a great council of their own to determine their best course of action. As many as 7,500 Lakotas from six of the seven subtribes gathered at the edge of the Black Hills along the Belle Fourche River. Among them were young men whose names would soon be well known among Lakotas and whites alike: Red Cloud, Crazy Horse, and Sitting Bull. It is probable that Gall also attended the council, although there is no reliable record of his participation. At the Great Teton Council, as it came to be known, the Lakotas pledged "not to permit further encroachments" upon their lands and lives by the whites.

While the Lakotas came to these resolutions in the West, government officials in the East were considering their own options for dealing with the crisis brewing on the plains. Some believed in "civilizing" the Indians— that is, teaching them to abandon the buffalo hunt, their religion, and their system of communal property, and to take up agriculture, Christianity, and the European practice of owning private property. Others did not believe it was possible to "civilize" the tribes and wanted simply to subdue them through war. Throughout these discussions, it remained clear that the U.S. government had no intention of halting the flow of settlers across Lakota lands.

By the time Gall was nearing 20, the situation had become even more tense. In 1858, gold was discovered in Colorado, and for the first time, the emigrants began to settle in Lakota territory instead of simply passing through it. A few years later, gold was also discovered at the headwaters of the Missouri in midwestern Montana, at the western edge of Lakota country. Thousands of ambitious gold diggers and their families passed through Lakota territory, cutting trails across the prairie and deep into the mountains. Nearest to Gall's territory was the path blazed by John Bozeman around 1862, which led

Gall's companion Sitting Bull, who pledged an oath of resistance at the Grand Council of the Tetons in 1857, would later become one of the most adamant defenders of the Lakota homelands. This portrait was made by a Canadian photographer in 1877.

straight through the Powder River country, where the Hunkpapas often hunted and wintered. Meanwhile, the buffalo were retreating farther and farther away from the Lakotas' traditional hunting grounds.

Most Lakotas came to believe that they had two choices. They could either yield to these changes and accept the rations offered by the government, or they could drive the settlers back. Because they did not agree on which path to take, their situation became still more complex. Those who favored resistance were angered not only by the white intruders, but by their own people and other plains tribes for giving in and accepting the whites' supplies. The Arikaras were among those who were growing dependent on the goods at the white trading posts. According to Bloody Knife, one day when he returned to the Hunkpapa camp to visit his father's people, he was stripped and beaten with coup sticks by Gall and other warriors.

By the early 1860s, tensions between the Lakotas and whites were simmering. Yet, as in the past, the Lakotas' main battles—the conflicts in which Gall's renown as a warrior grew—were fought against other Indians. In 1859, Gall fought beside Sitting Bull when the Hunkpapas were ambushed by Crows, and Sitting Bull's father, a powerful warrior, was killed. Gall himself later ambushed and killed several Arikaras, including Bloody Knife's brothers. For the next few years, at least, the problem of white intrusion remained secondary to the traditional conflicts that had occupied plains Indians for decades.

For the Lakotas' relatives to the east, however, hostilities with the whites had reached the crisis point. In 1862 in Minnesota, the Dakotas became involved in a violent uprising that left some 800 white men, women, and children dead. The U.S. Army was quick to retaliate: a contingent of soldiers under General Alfred Sully moved up the Missouri River; another, under General Henry Sibley, went to meet them. The generals commanded nearly 5,000 men and a battery of howitzers. Their goal was to "punish" the fleeing Dakotas, but they were willing to ignore distinctions and fight any Sioux who crossed their path.

3

▼ ▼ ▼

"THE WHITES RUIN
OUR COUNTRY"

Between 1863 and 1868, Gall and other prominent Lakota warriors frequently battled the U.S. Army along the Missouri and Yellowstone rivers. Gall's exploits during this period strengthened his reputation as a daring fighter and skilled strategist.

In the summer of 1863, Gall, Sitting Bull, and other Hunkpapa and Blackfoot Sioux leaders brought their camps east of the Missouri River, following the buffalo. The success of the hunt was crucial each summer, as the tribes relied on the buffalo meat to get them through the brutal plains winter. Fortunately, by the end of July, Gall and the others already had a huge stock of meat and furs. When a group of eastern Sioux fleeing Sibley's troops suddenly rushed into their camp, Gall and his companions were ready to defend their territory.

Following Lakota tradition, Gall and the other men decorated themselves for battle, painting their bodies and faces and donning the feathers that told of their exploits: white to denote a coup in battle; red to denote a wound. On July 26, the Sioux warriors entered their first engagement with U.S. soldiers. Having spotted a military camp on Dead Buffalo Lake in what is now North Dakota, they quietly positioned their horses in the hills around it. Then, in the style typical of Lakota warfare, they charged down the hills against their enemy—only to quickly retreat when they met the howitzers' shells. Thereafter, individual warriors darted toward the troops, trying to goad them into hand-to-hand combat, but the soldiers resisted. After

a few more advances and retreats, the battle ended, and the Lakotas withdrew to the west.

Two days later at Stony Lake, about 20 miles to the southwest, the Lakotas and the army clashed again. This time the Sioux approached the soldiers' camp in a single line five miles long. When they neared the camp, they parted, attempting to flank the baggage train, but they came under heavy fire and withdrew to the Missouri River. Sibley's men advanced on the Indians, who quickly constructed bullboats—rafts made from buffalo hides

After a bloody conflict between the Dakota Indians and Minnesota settlers in 1863, General Henry H. Sibley (pictured) helped lead a punitive expedition against the Sioux. Sibley defeated Lakota forces at Dead Buffalo and Stony lakes in present-day North Dakota.

pulled taut across willow frames. Although some of the Sioux were caught by the soldiers' gunfire, most managed to cross the river.

This was Gall's first conflict with U.S. soldiers. He had been fighting Crows, Arikaras, and other plains tribes for several years, but battling the whites was different, and it must have been sobering. The Lakotas had clearly been defeated; their traditional style of warfare and their bows, arrows, and muskets were no match for the army's strict organization, rifles, and cannons. Furthermore, they had retreated so quickly that they left behind their meat, furs, and equipment. The soldiers burned everything, and with the summer waning, the Lakotas had almost nothing to show for their long weeks of hunting. To Gall, who was by this time a husband, a father, and a prominent leader, responsible for the welfare of a large group of people, this loss must have been devastating. U.S. officials, meanwhile, were well aware of the hardships in store for the Indians. Sibley wrote that he hoped his campaign would cause many Sioux to "perish miserably in their utter destitution during the coming fall and winter."

For this season, the fighting was over. But the soldiers left a sign that the war was only beginning: they built Fort Sully on the Missouri River just south of the Cheyenne. This was the first indication that the U.S. Army planned to stay since Harney had placed troops at Fort Pierre in 1855. The army's goal was, as it had been for years, to protect white emigrants traveling into Lakota country, and ultimately to take control of Lakota territory. In the winter of 1863, the commissioner of Indian affairs, William Dole, declared that the United States—then in the throes of the Civil War—was now fighting, "in addition to the great rebellion, an Indian War of no mean proportion."

Indeed, the war to subjugate the Sioux continued. In

1864, the U.S. Army launched another campaign led by
General Sully. Its goal was to establish military posts
where the Missouri met the Heart and Yellowstone rivers,
thereby protecting both water and land routes to the
Montana gold mines. Sully's attitude toward the mission
was made clear in one of his first actions upon reaching
the Missouri. As he moved up the river with nearly 3,000
soldiers and many Indian scouts, one of his engineers was
killed by a group of Lakotas. The Sioux were swiftly
caught and killed. Then Sully ordered a sergeant to
impale their heads on poles and place them on a hill "as
a warning to all Indians who might travel that way."

*U.S. troops clash with
Indian warriors at a Lakota
encampment in 1863. In the
early battles between the
whites and the plains tribes,
the U.S. Army, with its
tight organization and
sophisticated weapons,
usually prevailed.*

When the expedition had passed the Little Missouri, Sully learned that a large group of Sioux—several thousand Hunkpapas, Sans Arcs, Blackfeet, Minneconjous, and Dakotas—were encamped not far away, and he resolved to pursue them. The Sioux had set up a large camp between the Heart and the Little Missouri rivers, where the land was made jagged and rough by wooded, brushy ravines and buttes that climbed to an elevation they called Tahchakuty, or Killdeer Mountain. When the Indians became aware of Sully's party, they called together their warriors. Gall and many others soon mounted their horses and ascended the mountain, where, brightly painted, they waited for the soldiers traveling toward them across the hot, dry plains. Because their numbers were large and their hilltop position was strong, the Sioux were confident. The women, children, and older men did not pack the tipis and goods for a hasty retreat, but gathered nearby to watch. On July 28, the battle began.

As before, the Sioux fought in their traditional style. Brave warriors rode out alone to draw the soldiers' fire; even a crippled man, Bear's Heart, rode into battle in a horse-drawn wagon to goad the soldiers. The warriors darted quickly on their ponies, trying to engage the soldiers in close combat. But, as in the battles at Dead Buffalo Lake and Stony Lake, bravery, bows and arrows, and muskets were simply not equal to cannons and rifles, nor to the explosives the soldiers threw into the ravines where the Sioux sought cover. The soldiers eventually attacked the Indian encampment itself, forcing the women, children, and older men to flee over the hills, leaving most of their belongings behind. More than a hundred Sioux died in the fighting; the army's losses, on the other hand, were minimal. Before leaving the Lakota camp, the soldiers burned it to the ground, destroying

buffalo robes, utensils, and, according to army reports, nearly 400,000 pounds of dried meat.

Sully continued on his way to Montana. Within a few days, his party reached the Dakota Bad Lands—a labyrinthine, desolate terrain of eroded buttes and narrow canyons, which Sully described as "hell with the fires burned out." This was land that few whites had ever seen, yet it was well known to the Lakotas, and they continued to track and harass Sully and his entourage. Still, the Indians could do no more than slow the army's progress, and Sully completed his mission, garrisoning Forts Union and Berthold—two trading posts along the upper Missouri River—and constructing a new post, Fort Rice, just south of Stony Lake.

After two summers of fighting, the Lakotas regarded the U.S. Army as a formidable foe. In the early winter of 1864, they learned of further evidence of the grim power of the whites: U.S. troops had attacked a camp of sleeping Cheyennes and Arapahos at Sand Creek, Colorado, killing and mutilating more than 130 Indians, most of them women and children. Many of the survivors of this brutal attack fled north, taking refuge among the Sioux.

The Sand Creek massacre angered the Lakotas and their allies; it also drew sharp criticism from U.S. citizens. In the cities along the eastern seaboard, the Lakotas and other Native Americans had always enjoyed a certain amount of public sympathy.

As the Civil War came to a close and the nation turned its attention westward, this popular support for the Indians continued to grow. Yet thousands of Americans, eager to reach the mines in Lakota territory, still demanded protection from the Sioux. Meanwhile, burdened by debt, the U.S. government began to regard the gold and silver that lay in these mines as vital to the nation's economy. In March 1865, Congress passed a joint resolu-

While leading an army expedition west to protect the Montana gold mines, General Alfred Sully (pictured) attacked a Lakota encampment at Killdeer Mountain near the Dakota Bad Lands. More than 100 Indians died in the ensuing battle.

tion in response to these competing interests: it would seek peace with the Sioux, but it would also build new roads to the mines in Montana. Later that year, General Sully was sent west to negotiate this "peace" with the plains Indians.

Two summers of devastating warfare had convinced many Indians that, as one Hunkpapa warrior put it, "the whites go wherever they want to, that nothing can stop them." Thus, in the fall of 1865, when Sully called a council at Fort Rice, a large number of Lakota, Cheyenne, and other tribal leaders attended and signed a new treaty allowing the government to enter their lands.

But several of the most renowned Lakota leaders, including Sitting Bull, Gall, and a prominent Oglala named Red Cloud, did not bother to attend Sully's meeting. In fact, when Sully had first arrived at Fort Rice earlier in the summer, Sitting Bull had fought back, making clear that he and his followers would reject the government's offer of peace. Sully's men had resisted this attack, and the warriors had retreated. Then, according to Sully, "a trusted Indian, half Arikara and half Hunkpapa, followed their trail across the badlands." Gall's old foe, Bloody Knife, had wasted little time in aligning himself with the U.S. military.

By this time, Gall had fought the white soldiers several times, and he had lost precious buffalo meat and hides. He did not have a personal stake in the fight, however, until that snowy night in December 1865 when he was bayoneted by U.S. soldiers at Fort Berthold. After this incident, his convictions gained depth and clarity.

That winter was a cold and hungry one. For the second year in a row, winter provisions had been destroyed, and Gall, despite his extraordinary fortitude, was weakened by his wounds. Yet he had not relinquished his role as leader, and he needed to keep his people fed. So when government officials arrived at Fort Laramie in the spring and summoned the Lakotas who had refused to come to Sully's council, Gall was probably among those who agreed to meet with them. He may have believed that the Lakotas should take what the white men were offering as payment—without having any intention of yielding to their requests for peace.

At the Fort Laramie council, treaty commissioner E. B. Taylor spoke of the gifts the resistant Lakotas were to receive, but he did not talk much of what they would be yielding in return: white emigrants' right of way along the Bozeman Trail, which branched off from the Platte River toward the northwest, crossing the Powder, Bighorn, and Yellowstone rivers, cutting directly through Lakota hunting grounds. Taylor knew that the Indians would not grant the emigrants' safe passage, yet he pretended to negotiate. Then, in the midst of the talks, Colonel Henry Carrington arrived with a battalion of infantry, under orders to build new forts along the Bozeman Trail, regardless of the meeting's outcome. Instantly, the head of the Oglalas, Red Cloud, stood up. "The Great Father sends us presents and wants us to sell him the road," he said, pointing angrily at the troops. "But White Chief goes with soldiers to steal the road before the Indians say Yes or No." Marching away with his followers, he told the council, "I am for war."

Red Cloud was not alone in his conviction. In the coming months, while he and his warriors repeatedly attacked the forts along the Bozeman Trail, Sitting Bull and the Hunkpapas focused on a new fort recently garrisoned by Sully: Fort Buford, at the confluence of the Yellowstone and Missouri rivers, deep in Hunkpapa territory. Gall, newly committed to defending his people's homeland, fought beside both leaders.

Unlike the fighting of the previous summers, these

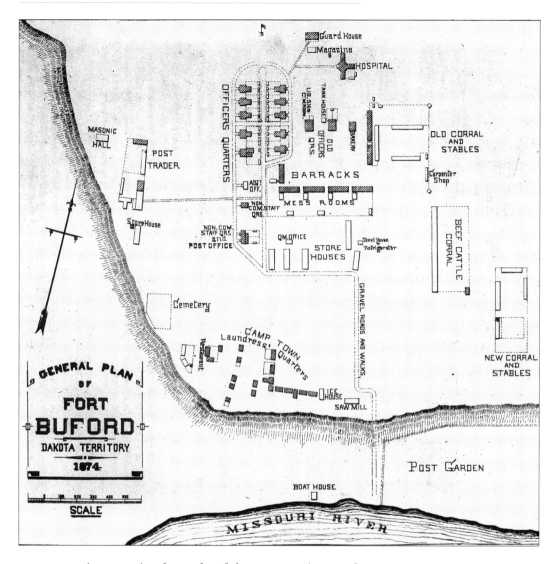

new campaigns consisted mostly of decoy operations and rapid raids. By the end of Red Cloud's War, as the hostilities along the Bozeman Trail became known, Gall had earned a reputation for his expertise in these areas. One of the most notorious conflicts occurred in December 1866 near Fort Phil Kearny, a newly built post in the Tongue River valley. There, on a clear, cold day, the Bighorn Mountains rising in the distance, a small party of warriors attacked a timber crew, who signaled to the

This 1874 diagram shows the layout of Fort Buford, a U.S. post situated near the confluence of the Yellowstone and Missouri rivers. Sitting Bull and Gall assaulted the fort repeatedly in December 1866.

fort for assistance. Several other Lakotas, led by a brave and enigmatic warrior named Crazy Horse, rode toward the fort to entice the soldiers out into the open. Captain William Fetterman and 80 soldiers soon poured forth to fend off the attackers, who galloped back over a nearby ridge. The soldiers followed, only to find on the other side of the ridge not the handful of warriors they had pursued but as many as 2,000. With arrows, hatchets, and spears, the Indians killed the entire company. For the Indians, the "Hundred-Soldiers-Killed-Fight" was a great victory; for the army, it was a terrible shock. General William Tecumseh Sherman, who now commanded all the troops on the plains, announced soon afterward, "We must act with vindictive earnestness against the Sioux, even to their extermination, men, women, and children."

Meanwhile, Sitting Bull and Gall launched raids against Fort Buford, firing at the soldiers with artillery and setting alight their wood piles, which had been carefully prepared for the upcoming winter. By the winter of 1866, Gall was recognized by many soldiers as "the fighting cock of the Sioux." At the age of 26, he was an imposing man. According to Joseph Taylor, a trapper who was friendly with the Indians, "Gall stood in his moccasins near six feet tall, a frame of bone, with the full breast of a gladiator and bearing of one born to command. No senator of old Rome ever draped his toga with more becoming grace to the dignity of his position in the Forum, than did Gall in his chief's robe at an Indian council."

The attacks on Forts Buford, Phil Kearny, and nearby C. F. Smith continued relentlessly for nearly a year. Finally, in July 1867, Congress passed a bill to make a new peace with the Indians—or, as an amendment to the bill put it, "to conquer a peace." In the fall a new peace commission, which included General Sherman, came to Fort Laramie to talk with Lakota leaders. "The railroads

are coming," Sherman sternly told the Lakotas, "and you cannot stop [them] any more than you can stop the sun or moon. You must decide; you must submit. This is not a peace commission only; it is also a war commission." Some of the Lakotas were cowed by Sherman's threats, but Red Cloud remained firm, replying, "If the Great Father kept white men out of my country, then peace would last forever." Red Cloud, Crazy Horse, Gall, and

Government agents gather beside a young Lakota girl to commemorate negotiations at Fort Laramie in 1867.

their followers intensified their raids. In one November attack, some historians believe, Gall was wounded.

Finally, in 1868, the United States decided it had had enough of the trouble on the Bozeman Trail. The Indians' attacks had been so intense that almost no one could get through. Moreover, the new railroads promised to open up shorter routes to the Montana gold. That spring, the peace commission returned to Lakota territory to declare that it would give up rights to the trail. But Red Cloud—keeping an eye on the Bozeman forts from a hilltop—sent word to the officials that he would not stop fighting until the posts had disappeared.

The commission continued to bargain. In addition to its offer of peace, the treaty involved the creation of two huge Indian reservations, one in Oklahoma Territory and the other in present-day South Dakota. These reservations would enable non-Indians to move through or settle the other prairie land, satisfying the country's economic goals. Yet they would also allow the Indians to keep some of their land, satisfying those who were sympathetic to the Indians' cause. Perhaps the ultimate aim of this treaty, however, was the "civilization" of the Indians: on the new reservations, they were to give up hunting for farming.

Gall, who was asked to address the commission at one point during the negotiations, arrived at Fort Laramie in his war outfit, carrying his rifle across his arm. Speaking on behalf of Sitting Bull and other Lakota leaders, he told the officials:

> This is our land and our home. We have no exact boundaries, but the graves of the Sioux nation mark our possessions. Wherever they are found the land is ours. We were born naked, and have been taught to hunt and live on the game. You tell us that we must learn to farm, live in one house, and take on your ways. Suppose the people living be-

yond the great sea should come and tell you that you must stop farming and kill your cattle, and take your houses and lands, what would you do? Would you not fight them?

At another point in the discussion, Gall again spoke, revealing wounds on his chest:

> Your hands are red with blood, you see the bleeding wounds on my breast. . . . Not until this fort is burned down and I can see my foot prints in the dead ashes will I believe what you say. Not until the wounds I carry are healed, the lands that belong to us restored, will I sign a treaty with you.

Indeed, Gall never signed that treaty; nor did any of the other leaders who had been directing the recent fighting. In a fresh effort to win their approval, the government sent a special envoy who was well liked by the Lakotas, a Jesuit missionary named Pierre-Jean De Smet, to persuade them to attend a new meeting at Fort Rice in July.

Father De Smet, whom the Lakotas called "Black Robe" for his long garments, was a gentle, courageous man. On June 19, he reached the Hunkpapa camp near the junction of the Yellowstone and Powder rivers, and Gall led a party of brightly painted and clothed Hunkpapa warriors and chiefs out to greet him. The meeting began the next day in a huge council lodge. Gall and other important war chiefs sat in the front on buffalo robes, while hundreds of tribe members crowded behind them. A ceremonial pipe was passed, and then both sides spoke. De Smet genuinely longed for an end to the bloodshed, as did the Lakotas. And they were prepared to make peace, but only if the whites agreed to leave their lands and let them live in freedom. The Indians made no concessions at this council, but after long debate, Sitting Bull, their main spokesman, agreed to send a delegation of chiefs to the treaty meeting, with Gall as its leader.

Arriving at Fort Rice on July 2, Gall and his party

Pierre-Jean De Smet, a Jesuit missionary whose strength and compassion inspired Indian goodwill from the Great Lakes region to the Pacific Northwest, visited Gall's camp in the summer of 1868 to encourage peace between the Lakotas and the U.S. government.

were offered a treaty identical to the one that had been signed by lesser tribesmen earlier in the year. Like most of the government's treaties, it was laden with legalities, and the Indians probably understood very little of it. It established a Great Sioux Reservation in the western half of what is now South Dakota—a tiny fraction of the Lakotas' traditional lands, and an area that excluded the Hunkpapas' hunting grounds. The treaty also stated that the Indians would relinquish the "right to occupy permanently the territory outside their reservation" but retain the right to hunt on specified "unceded territory," "so long as the buffalo may range thereon in such numbers as to justify the chase"; that the U.S. could lay rail and make wagon roads on the reservation; and that the Sioux were to move to agencies—government-run communities on reservation land—where they would receive rations for a time and adopt the "civilization" of whites. The Indians were told that refusal to sign the treaty would result in a war in which thousands would die and the rest would be left with no land.

Gall responded to the commission's proposal with a passionate speech:

> The whites ruin our country. If we make peace, the military posts on this Missouri River must be removed and the steamboats stopped from coming up here. . . . The annuities you speak of we don't want. . . . You talk of peace. If we make peace, you will not hold it. We told the good Black Robe who has been to our camp that we do not like these things. I have been sent here by my people to see and hear what you have got to say. My people told me to get powder and ball, and I want that.

His address completed, Gall waited for the other chiefs to take their turn. Then, having declared his terms for peace, he marched to the table where the papers lay and signed the treaty under the name Man-that-Goes-in-the-Middle. The other chiefs followed.

As with so many U.S.–Indian treaties, what the Indians intended when they signed this document was very different from what the U.S. representatives were calling for. Gall signed the treaty as though it were a promise: if the government halted its aggressions, he and the Hunkpapas would halt theirs. According to the United States, however, those who signed the treaty accepted its terms and would abide by them.

Gall did not understand what his signature meant to the whites, but even if he had, his signature by no means represented the agreement of all the Hunkpapas, as the government agents well knew. Nevertheless, the Treaty of 1868 had been signed, an act that was to have severe consequences.

4

THE THIEVES' ROAD

For several years after the signing of the Treaty of 1868, there was relative peace in Lakota territory. While some Lakotas cooperated with the government and moved to the new agencies, many others, including Gall, Sitting Bull, and Crazy Horse, remained in the "unceded territory" of the Powder and Bighorn river valleys, hunting buffalo.

At about this time, the "true Lakotas," as those who avoided the reservations were called, made an unusual change in their social and political structure. Having attended a number of U.S.–Indian councils, they may have realized that their traditional system of government could cause conflicts when it came to signing treaties, because it recognized many chiefs of equal rank. To remedy this problem, they decided to elect one head chief, and for this position they chose Sitting Bull. Gall took part in the decision and in the elaborate ceremony that followed.

Gall's own status as a chief has never been clearly defined. Lakota chiefs did not wield singular authority. In civil affairs, they led by example and tried to represent the will of their people. Likewise, in battle, war chiefs did not command their followers the way white generals did, but instead served as role models. By the late 1860s,

A work party cuts a path for the Northern Pacific Railroad, chartered to run from St. Paul, Minnesota, straight through the Lakota hunting grounds, to the West Coast in Washington Territory.

Gall was widely admired, for throughout the years of fighting soldiers in the field and raiding their forts, he had proved himself a brave and intelligent warrior. "You can't help but feel very friendly when you see him," a man who knew him, Robert Higheagle, once remarked. "You are not afraid to talk to him. Sitting Bull was so reserved it was not easy to approach him like it was Gall." Unlike Sitting Bull, whose authority extended into civil and even spiritual matters, Gall was primarily a war chief. Yet he also served as an adviser to Sitting Bull, his older "brother," on all kinds of issues affecting the tribe.

The Laramie River flows by an encampment near Red Cloud Agency, where many of the Oglala, Minneconjou, and Brulé Sioux settled after the Treaty of 1868 was signed. Gall, Sitting Bull, and their followers avoided the agencies and moved their camps farther north, where they were able to live and hunt without government interference.

Gall's views tended to be militant. Around 1870, a young, half-white, half-Polynesian outlaw named Frank Grouard arrived in Sitting Bull's camp, and Gall, suspicious of all white men, advised Sitting Bull to kill him. The older chief, however, thinking that Grouard looked like one of his own people, chose instead to adopt him. Sitting Bull's decision was to play an important role in the U.S.–Indian conflicts that lay ahead.

With Sitting Bull, Crazy Horse, and the other true Lakotas, Gall spent the early 1870s drifting back and forth between northern Montana and the prairies south of the Yellowstone. This vast range, which had been won through decades of warfare with the Crows, Gall and the others now considered the Lakota heartland. There the true Lakotas encountered fewer whites than they had seen in the 1860s; they also had less frequent contact with their tribesmen at the agencies, who were beginning to submit to a life of white-style farming and education. The hunting bands pledged to resist such changes, although when winter was especially harsh even Gall sometimes came to the agencies for rations. Meanwhile, as Sherman had promised, the railroads were coming, and they were to have a deadly effect on the buffalo hunt.

For in July 1864, Congress had chartered the "construction of a railroad and telegraph-line from Lake Superior to the Puget Sound," promising to "extinguish . . . the Indian titles to all lands falling under the operation of this act." By 1873, the new Northern Pacific Railroad line had reached Bismarck, in present-day North Dakota, where the Heart River meets the Missouri. It was then to continue west, following the Yellowstone River north of the unceded hunting grounds of Gall, Sitting Bull, and the true Lakotas.

By this time, most Indians already knew what it would mean to have a railroad cutting through their lands. In

1869, the Union Pacific railway line had been completed. It ran west along the North Platte River just south of Fort Laramie, and the plains tribes had seen how the trains sent the buffalo stampeding and brought scores of miners and settlers. So in September 1871, when a railroad survey team, escorted by a large company of U.S. troops under General J. N. G. Whistler, launched an expedition west from Fort Rice toward the Yellowstone, the hunting bands grew wary. The Indians slowed the progress of the approaching surveyors by setting great swaths of prairie grass on fire.

The following summer, Gall and his followers joined

This 1832 painting by George Catlin shows Indians fleeing a prairie fire. The Lakotas believed that burning the dry grasslands encouraged new growth; they also set fires to threaten their enemies.

other Lakotas at a huge encampment near the Powder River to hunt and celebrate the Sun Dance. They were planning a raid on their enemies the Crows when suddenly word came of troops in the area. In fact, two surveying expeditions were approaching, one marching east under the command of Major Eugene Baker, the other moving west under Colonel David Stanley. The two were to meet at the Powder River.

On the morning of August 14, Sitting Bull, Gall, Crazy Horse, and several hundred Sioux and Cheyenne warriors tracked down Baker's expedition and attacked the party, leaving several men dead. The surveyors were so frightened that they insisted on redirecting their survey, and the party retreated. Meanwhile, Gall, scouting the area, discovered Stanley's party coming from the other direction.

With Stanley were nearly 600 men, several Gatling guns (primitive machine guns), and one brass 12-pound cannon. On August 16, Gall and fewer than 30 warriors descended on them from the woods. Galloping straight through their camp, the Indians chased down a fleeing engineer, exchanged fire briefly with the soldiers, and retreated across the Powder River. Then, dropping his rifle on the riverbank, Gall shouted across the water to Stanley, loudly asking what the soldiers were doing in Lakota country, although he was well aware of their plans. When Stanley told him, the war chief asked how much the whites intended to pay for the privilege of building a railroad. Nothing, Stanley replied. Gall then shouted that he would "bring all the bands" of Lakotas and give the soldiers a "big fight." Stanley stepped back, and there was a quick exchange of gunfire before Gall and his band withdrew downstream.

Gall was soon joined by Sitting Bull and several hundred warriors, who shadowed the expedition back

Flamboyant Civil War veteran George Armstrong Custer was one of the most controversial figures in the history of the U.S.–Indian wars. Craving fame above all else, Custer once boasted that his regiment could "whip all the Indians in the Northwest."

across the Bad Lands and down the Heart River, engaging the troops in combat at brief intervals. As Stanley and his men neared Fort Rice, Gall attacked a party that had left the main contingent, killing two lieutenants and Stanley's black cook.

In the end, despite the Lakotas' attempts to impede them, the expeditions were successful. Yet Stanley was angry to note how many of the "hostile Sioux" had acquired sophisticated weapons—Winchester and Henry repeating rifles—from the traders in the region. He noted with particular irritation that " 'The Gall,' the first Indian to lead a war party to fire on us last summer, traded twenty-three [buffalo] robes for Henry cartridges and carried out with him three kegs of powder." The Lakotas were beginning to arm themselves for war.

That same summer, Gall, Sitting Bull, and Crazy Horse launched attacks on a new post, Fort Abraham Lincoln, built to protect the railway lines at the confluence of the Heart and Missouri rivers. The Lakotas fought with such persistence that a crew of Arikara scouts was hired to help track and repel them, and by the fall of 1872, the head of military operations on the plains, Philip Sheridan, had ordered a cavalry regiment to bolster U.S. forces in the region. The renowned Seventh Cavalry arrived the following spring under the command of a man destined to play a legendary role in the history of U.S.–Indian relations: George Armstrong Custer. Impressed by his long, reddish blond curls, the Lakotas called him Long Hair.

In June 1873, when the Seventh Cavalry had arrived, Custer accompanied Stanley on another expedition into the Powder River country. About 2,000 men, even more animals, 40 scouts, and close to 300 wagons took part in this venture—a colossal invasion of the Lakota heartland. By August, the party had reached the Yellowstone and was moving north toward the Tongue, with Custer and an advance cavalry unit scouting ahead. It was not long before Gall, Sitting Bull, and a sizeable band of Hunkpapas and Minneconjous spotted Custer's unit. Immediately, some 100 warriors, with Gall in the lead, set out to decoy Custer, crawling through timber, down ravines, and along the riverbanks until they were near the camp. Custer, however, saw through the trap and held the Indians off until the rest of the troops arrived. Then he followed the withdrawing Lakotas to the Yellowstone near a rocky outcropping called Pompey's Pillar, where the Indians quickly forded the deep river on bullboats.

The next day more warriors—Minneconjous, Sans Arcs, Oglalas, and Cheyennes—arrived at the Lakota camp. Encouraged by these reinforcements, Sitting Bull and Gall stood on the bank of the Yellowstone and taunted the soldiers, who fired back furiously. To further provoke the troops, Gall rode back and forth before them, dressed in a brilliant scarlet robe and a warbonnet; bullets whizzed past him, but he remained unharmed. Some Lakotas crossed the river to engage in hand-to-hand combat, but the arrival of Stanley and his cannon drove them back, ending the battle. Despite the Lakotas' efforts, the members of this massive survey crew, like those who had gone before them, managed to complete their mission.

Indeed, by 1873 the two factors that most threatened the Lakota way of life—the reservation and the railroad—were being shoehorned into Lakota territory. That year, a depression swept the country, putting a stop to the work on the railroad. Ultimately, however, the nation's financial troubles caused the whites to penetrate even deeper into Lakota lands. This time, the government set its sights on the Black Hills, a shadowy range that towered 4,000 feet above the plains. There had been rumors of gold in this region since the early 1800s, and though such reports had never been confirmed, to a nation in economic distress their appeal was irresistible. U.S. officials decided to fund an exploratory expedition into the hills, and Custer volunteered to lead it.

The Black Hills were beloved by the Lakotas. Not only were they revered as the home of the gods, but they were full of game, fruit, timber for tipi poles, and herbs for medicine. The Sioux regarded the hills as a final refuge; when all the buffalo were gone, they believed, their people could always go to the Black Hills, or Pa Sapa, which would provide for them. Indeed, even within the

terms of the Treaty of 1868, the Black Hills were
off-limits to white intrusion. Government officials were
aware of this problem, but by reinterpreting some of the
treaty's obscure phrases, they found a way to defend
the project. They also knew they could always point to
the behavior of the Sioux to justify their actions. For, far
from settling peacefully at the agencies, the hunting
bands had continued to harass the newcomers, stampeding 90 mules from Fort Lincoln in April and attacking
the villages of enemy Arikaras and others at Fort Berthold
in May. Officials asserted that the Sioux were not keeping
up their end of the treaty, and so there was no need for
the government to honor its own promises. This argu-
ment, of course, disregarded the fact that many Lakota
bands had never signed the treaty in the first place.

Just as the nation's expansion west had continued
inexorably through the middle of the century, its economic requirements were not to be ignored now. As a
reporter for the *Sioux City Journal* put it, "This [expedi-
tion] will be the wedge which will open the coveted
country. Even if there be no gold worth delving for in
the Black Hills, it is known positively that there is pine
timber and coal in almost inexhaustible supplies, and the
presence of these valuable articles of themselves is
sufficient cause for the throwing open to civilization of
the coveted region."

In July 1874, Custer led 1,000 men with a supply train
of 110 wagons, about 2,000 animals, and a band of Arikara
scouts—Bloody Knife among them—from Fort Lincoln
toward the Black Hills, following a path the Lakotas
would later call the Thieves' Road. The nearly 1,000-mile
expedition to the hills and back took place without
significant opposition from the Lakotas, and before long
Custer was wiring back reports detailing the natural
wonder of the place—the richness of the soil, the quantity

of elk and antelope, the wonderful abundance of flowers and other foliage, and most important, the "gold at the grass roots."

Custer's news electrified the nation, and within weeks, miners were scrambling to reach the Black Hills. The government, alarmed for the miners' safety and still uncertain what to do about the Sioux, at first ordered the military to turn the newcomers away. But in the summer of 1875, when a second expedition confirmed Custer's reports, officials knew that it would be impossible to control the flood of prospectors and that the Lakotas' rights to the land would have to be extinguished. In his

Members of Custer's 1874 expedition to the Black Hills gather at their camp near the Yellowstone River.

annual report, General Sheridan argued that breaking the Treaty of 1868 would really be the best for all concerned, writing: "There is true humanity in making the reservations reasonably small by dividing them into tracts for the heads of families, making labor gradually compulsory, and even compelling children to go to school." Government agents were soon traveling to Lakota territory to negotiate the purchase of the Black Hills.

Late in the summer of 1875, government agents invited the Lakotas to a council being held near the Sioux agencies. Although the hunting bands' best-known leaders refused to go, about 400 Oglalas attended the meeting in a spectacular way. Stripped and painted for war, they charged down the bluffs around the council site, firing rifles into the air and declaring that they would shoot anyone who signed a treaty. The council quickly dissolved.

Believing that peaceful efforts had failed, the government resorted to other methods of acquiring the Black Hills. First, President Ulysses S. Grant announced that the military would no longer prevent miners from entering the region. Then, in November, E. C. Watkins, an inspector reporting to the commissioner of Indian affairs, offered U.S. officials justification for a more active assault on the Lakotas. Commenting on the activities of Sitting Bull and other members of the hunting bands, he concluded that the "only policy worthy an enlightened, Christian nation" was to "whip them into subjection. They richly merit the punishment for their incessant warfare on friendly tribes, their continuous thieving, and their numerous murders of white settlers and their families, or white men wherever found unarmed." Seizing on Watkins's arguments, on December 3, the president issued an ultimatum: unless the hunting bands came into the agencies by January 31, 1876, the U.S. Army would take action against them.

5

"IT MADE MY HEART BAD"

In December 1875, Gall, Sitting Bull, and other Hunkpapas were wintering on the Yellowstone near the mouth of the Powder River. Most likely, they were unconcerned when they heard that the government was ordering them to go to the agencies. By this time, they were used to being summoned to agency councils; usually these meetings meant that the government wanted their lands. They had no interest in meeting with the whites at the moment, and besides, it was much too cold to travel. Some of the Indians, therefore, sent word that they would come in the spring, when they had buffalo robes to trade. Even if the Sioux had understood the seriousness of the ultimatum, most of them would not have been able to make it through the thick snowfall and bitter cold before the government's deadline.

When February came and almost none of the hunting bands had appeared at the agencies, U.S. officials announced that the Powder River Sioux had defied the order. Although the Indians did not know it, they were now at war with the United States.

The fighting began one frigid March morning, when U.S. troops stormed a camp of sleeping Cheyennes just north of the mouth of the Little Powder River. As the

West Point graduate George Crook (pictured), an experienced Indian fighter, played a leading role in the U.S. war against the Sioux, declared on February 1, 1876.

Indians rushed from their beds to defend themselves, the soldiers set fire to their lodges, burning at least half of them to the ground. Few of the Cheyennes were killed in this surprise attack, but they were left without food, clothing, or shelter. Struggling through the ice and snow, they somehow managed to reach the camps of Crazy Horse, Sitting Bull, and Gall on an elevation between the Powder and the Little Missouri rivers. Gall soon learned that the soldiers had been led to the Cheyenne encampment by an astute white scout: Frank Grouard. No doubt this prompted Gall to remember the advice he had given Sitting Bull years before and to reaffirm his hatred and suspicion of white intruders.

Soon after the attack, about 235 lodges of Hunkpapas, Oglalas, and Cheyennes met in council to decide how to respond. A Cheyenne chief named Two Moons later recalled, "All agreed to stay together and fight." At this point, however, they made no plans for an offensive. Spring was approaching, and this was the usual time for the various bands of Lakotas to congregate for the summer's hunting and festivities. Sitting Bull, Crazy Horse, Gall, and other Lakota leaders believed that when all of the hunting bands came together, they would have no more trouble from the whites. As a Cheyenne named Wooden Leg put it, "We supposed that the combined camps would frighten off the soldiers. We hoped thus to be freed from their annoyance. Then we could separate again into tribal bands and resume our quiet wandering."

The campaign against the Sioux had officially begun on February 1. Following orders from Sheridan, General George Crook was to approach Lakota territory from the south; meanwhile, Colonel John Gibbon would move in from Fort Ellis in the west, and Colonel Custer and General Alfred Terry would approach from Fort Lincoln in the east.

Frank Grouard, a drifter who was found trespassing in Lakota territory in 1869, lived with the Hunkpapas for three years as Sitting Bull's adopted brother. He later betrayed the Indians, becoming an informer for the U.S. Army.

By June, some 3,000 Indians, including perhaps 800 warriors, had gathered around Sitting Bull, Crazy Horse, and Gall. Many of them had come from the agencies, where rations had run out, leaving them with little choice but to return to their old livelihood of hunting. The great encampment moved with the buffalo herds, and by the early summer, it had left the area between the Little Missouri and Powder rivers, crossed the Powder and the

Horses gather at a stream near a Lakota encampment photographed in the late 19th century. In the summer of 1876, some 3,000 plains Indians assembled near the Powder River to hunt and celebrate the Sun Dance.

Tongue, and reached the lower Rosebud River. The Indians would camp in a location for a few days, until their ponies and campfires had consumed the available brush, and then move on. The encampment was led by the Cheyennes and trailed by the Hunkpapas—the largest and strongest tribes—and also included Oglalas, Brulés, Minneconjous, Sans Arcs, and Blackfeet, each tribe camping in its own circle, with tipis opening to the east. The Lakotas were engaging in their usual summer activities; they were not pursuing war. But as they approached the Rosebud River, scouts riding both north and south in search of buffalo instead spotted U.S. troops, confirming Sioux suspicions that a large campaign was being launched against them.

The Lakotas were not alarmed by their discovery, for at the time they were feeling particularly strong. The hunting had been good, and their population was larger than it had ever been. Over the past few years, they had waged successful raids on the army's forts, and just a few months earlier they had blocked the sale of the Black Hills. Rich in ponies, buffalo meat, and furs, and enjoying an enormous gathering of their people in their own heartland, the Lakotas felt they were ready to counter any offensive the U.S. Army might wage against them. Their fighting spirit was fueled by the year's most spectacular celebration, the Sun Dance.

The Lakotas held this great ceremony in early June. Young Hunkpapa women selected the sacred tree around which the warriors and chiefs would dance, elders carried the tree to the dance circle, and members of every tribe in the encampment gathered there to watch. The focal point of the dance was Sitting Bull, the supreme chief of the Lakotas. Gouging 50 pieces of skin from each of his arms, he pledged a sacrifice to Wakan Tanka, then danced for 18 hours around the sacred pole. Finally he collapsed, fell into a trance, and witnessed a vision of a vast army of soldiers falling head first into an Indian village. As he witnessed this vision, Sitting Bull said that he heard a great voice say, "These soldiers do not possess ears. They are to die, but you are not supposed to take their spoils." Gall and Crazy Horse, who were among those who watched Sitting Bull's sacrifice and dance and heard his prophecy, were certain that they would soon meet the whites in battle.

A week later, while moving up the Rosebud, the Lakotas encountered General Crook's column of more than 1,000 men, 120 wagons, and 1,000 pack mules, and on June 17, a large party of Oglalas, Brulés, Hunkpapas, and Cheyennes descended on the company. The two sides fought fiercely for hours, and by the end of the battle, although Crook's casualties were somewhat lower, his men had taken a severe beating and were forced to retreat. This had been a great fight for the Indians, who had been outnumbered more than two to one. Celebrating their victory, they moved down Reno Creek toward the Little Bighorn River. In the Valley of the Greasy Grass, as they called this area, their numbers swelled even further, as more agency Indians arrived to hunt. Their camp now comprised some 1,000 lodges and 7,000 people, including 1,800 warriors. Thus augmented, the Indians waited for another encounter, one grand enough to fulfill Sitting Bull's prophecy.

On June 24, learning of antelope to the north and west, the Indians headed down the Little Bighorn. After a day of traveling, they set up camp, spreading out for about three miles down the west side of the river, with the Hunkpapas, as usual, at the rear. To the west were low hills where the ponies grazed; to the east the cold river was lined with cottonwood trees. Beyond the river, bluffs rose as high as 300 feet, while far to the south of the village rose the snowcapped Bighorn Mountains. That evening, the village was filled with the sounds and smells of cooking, of hides and meat being prepared, and of hunting weapons being cleaned and sharpened. Neither Gall, huddled with his wives and children in his tipi, nor any of the other Lakota leaders had any idea that their greatest clash with the U.S. military was only hours away.

On May 17, a column led by Terry and Custer had left Fort Lincoln for Bighorn country. The column was made up of all 12 companies of the Seventh Cavalry, three companies of infantry, and 40 Arikara scouts: altogether, more than 900 men. With them were three Gatling guns, a train of 150 wagons, and an immense herd of cattle and mules. Among the Arikara scouts under Custer's command was Bloody Knife. By this time, he had become a trusted ally of Custer, who had given him a silver medal and promoted him from enlisted auxiliary to civilian scout. On June 21, Terry and Custer met with Gibbon, who was coming from the west, where the Rosebud feeds into the Yellowstone.

Terry was by this time at odds with both Custer and his other commanding officer, Major Marcus Reno. Both had shown a likeliness to disobey orders if the opportunity arose for a glorious victory under their own command. Custer, in fact, had earlier been court-martialed, and now he told Colonel William Ludlow that he planned to cut loose from Terry and gain all the credit for defeating the "hostiles" himself. To someone else he declared that his Seventh Cavalry could "whip all the Indians in the northwest." On June 22, Terry and Gibbon headed up the Yellowstone and Bighorn rivers to reach the Little Bighorn; Custer, Reno, and the Seventh Cavalry, meanwhile, headed up the Rosebud River valley to find the Sioux camp and drive it north toward Terry and Gibbon. They were to coordinate their attacks on June 26.

After two days, Custer found a freshly deserted Sioux campsite, and that night, Bloody Knife scouted the trail. The following morning, scouts reported that on the other

side of the divide between the Rosebud and the Little Bighorn they saw rising smoke and pony herds—signs of a large Sioux encampment. Although Bloody Knife warned his commander that there were enough Sioux to keep the army fighting for several days, according to Lieutenant Edward Godfrey, Custer laughingly declared that his men "could get through them in one day." He

Major Marcus Reno launched the Battle of the Little Bighorn on July 25, 1876. Pummeling Reno's troops with arrows and bullets, Gall and his warriors drove them into the nearby woods, then rushed north to confront Custer.

decided to advance immediately, before the Sioux camp could travel—and before Terry and Gibbon could coordinate their own attack.

Custer's column proceeded over the divide. Five companies followed Custer north and then split into three factions, one continuing on under Custer, another following Captain Frederick Benteen, and a third staying behind to guard the pack train. Reno turned to the left with three companies—including 16 Arikara scouts under Bloody Knife's command—to initiate the attack from the south. Custer told Reno to advance rapidly and that he and his men would soon be there to support him.

The Indians, meanwhile, were absorbed in the activities of a hot, drowsy day. Women and children swam in the river or hunted for berries and roots. Some men slept after a late night of festivities, while others fished or tended the ponies. One group of women, however, decided to climb the bluffs east of the river, and when they reached the top they spotted Custer's troops approaching. Immediately they cried the alarm: "They are charging, the chargers are coming!" All through the encampment, women packed up tipis, while men leapt to action, painting themselves and grabbing their ponies, some hurrying their families to a safer position in the hills to the west or north. The air was full of dust, shouting, singing, and the sound of bullets cracking through tipi poles. The Hunkpapas, at the southern end of the encampment, lay in the first line of attack.

Reno's soldiers poured down the Little Bighorn valley, a party of Arikaras branching off in pursuit of a herd of Hunkpapa ponies. In almost no time, a band of Hunkpapa warriors appeared from a ravine. They made no sign of yielding their ground the way Reno seemed to have expected, instead letting loose a blizzard of arrows and bullets. Reno's men dismounted and formed a skirmish line—a defensive action indicating Reno was expecting backup—while Arikara scouts rode on ahead of the soldiers, firing into the Hunkpapa tipis. Among the first tipis struck was Gall's, and his two wives and three children were killed. "It made my heart bad," he said later. "After that I killed all my enemies with the hatchet." A large Hunkpapa war party soon charged the line of soldiers. In the lead, astride a black pony and wearing nothing but war paint, was Gall.

The Hunkpapas soon drew reinforcements from a party of Oglalas, and Reno, seeing no sign of Custer and the promised backup, quickly retreated into the timber alongside the river. There, with his men taking refuge behind trees as they tried to shoot at the warriors around them, Reno attempted to reorganize his troops into fighting

This drawing by White Bird, a Lakota artist, represents the two main theaters of action in the Battle of the Little Bighorn. While a party of Hunkpapas bears down on Reno's men (right), another Lakota force charges on troops fighting under Custer.

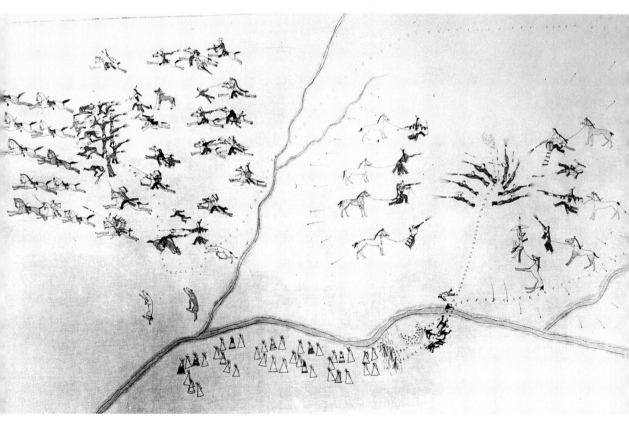

columns. But as he prepared to charge again, with Bloody Knife at his side, gunfire rang out—and Bloody Knife collapsed, a bullet in his head, which spattered Reno's face with brains and blood. Reno and his men recoiled at this and galloped back up the valley and across the Little Bighorn to take a safer position on a bluff. Forty soldiers had been killed and about 30 wounded or left behind. Although less than an hour had passed since the beginning of the battle, Reno must have been wondering what had happened to Custer.

As Reno retreated, women and children from the great encampment crossed the battleground, shooting those soldiers who lay wounded and stripping and mutilating the bodies of the dead. Meanwhile, Gall and his war party raced to cut off Reno. Before they had proceeded far, however, a warrior named Iron Cedar rushed up to Gall and informed him that more soldiers were approaching from the north. Gall spread the word among his men, then turned and headed in the direction of Custer. After leaving Reno, Custer had ridden north along the bluffs paralleling the east bank of the Little Bighorn, then spotted the massive Indian camp. Sending a courier to tell Benteen to hurry his companies back, Custer had prepared to attack. As his men dismounted, however, the Lakotas charged across the river and up Medicine Tail coulee toward them. Gall later described the action: "[The white soldiers] fought on foot. One man held the horses while the others shot the guns. We tried to kill the holders, and then by waving blankets and shouting we scared the horses down that coulee, where the Cheyenne women caught them."

With their horses and ammunition gone, Custer's troops fell into disarray. According to one Oglala woman, the Indians "acted just like they were driving buffalo to a good place where they could be easily slaughtered."

Gall and his warriors held a position protected by a slope, which enabled them to jump up, shoot, and quickly hide again, drawing and wasting the soldiers' fire. At a shout from Gall, a mass of warriors leapt up in unison, cried out, and rushed toward the soldiers. Custer's men were falling by the dozens; when a group of them broke off and ran toward the river, they were quickly chased into a ravine and killed. Meanwhile, another group of soldiers reached the top of the ravine. They "were loading and fighting," Gall later said, "but they could not hit the warriors in the gully and the ravine. The dust and smoke was black as evening. Once in a while we could see the soldiers through the dust, and finally we charged through

Sioux and Cheyenne warriors crush the Seventh Cavalry as Custer makes his celebrated "Last Stand," in a painting by Theodore B. Pitman.

them with our ponies. When we had done this . . . the fight was over." In less than one hour, George Armstrong Custer and every one of his men lay dead.

The Lakotas then headed south to confront Reno, who by this time had been joined by Benteen and the pack train. Gall and his warriors stayed along the river, knowing that the soldiers would eventually be forced to seek water. On the following day, they surrounded and attacked Reno's troops. But then Gall saw what he called "the big dust," which signified the approach of more white soldiers, so he and his warriors soon withdrew to the southwest.

When they had reached a safe camp, they mourned their dead, then celebrated the greatest victory they had ever known. Their conquest, however, was not entirely a happy one. Although Sitting Bull's prophecy had been fulfilled, his people had ignored its warning by plundering the bodies of the fallen soldiers. According to Sitting Bull, this meant that the Indians would be cursed with a fatal desire for white people's goods.

Terry and Gibbon soon reached the site of the Battle of the Little Bighorn and reported the terrible news to Washington in early July. The nation—celebrating its centennial—was both shocked and angered by the news of Custer's fall. A new, even more furious assault on the "hostile" Sioux began.

6

THE LAST DAYS OF THE BUFFALO

Colonel Nelson A. Miles, a former crockery salesman with high military ambitions, tracked the Sioux after the U.S. defeat at the Little Bighorn.

After the Battle of the Little Bighorn, the Lakotas continued their summer hunting, crossing to the Rosebud, turning east toward the Tongue River, and then heading northeast up the Powder. Generals Crook and Terry set out after them. Their progress was slow, however, for the two officers were often at odds. Moreover, their troops and animals were worn out and their information on the Indians' whereabouts was unreliable. Late in August, Crook split off from Terry and marched toward the Black Hills for supplies. Near the head of the Moreau River at a spot called Slim Buttes, his advance contingent discovered a Lakota encampment. The soldiers attacked the camp at dawn on September 9, killing several women and children, and then proceeded to the Black Hills.

That fall, the war against the Sioux took on new dimensions. Making no distinction between the Sioux who had fought with the hunting bands that summer and those who had remained at the agencies, Sheridan ordered the Indians at Standing Rock, Cheyenne River, Red Cloud, and Spotted Tail agencies to turn in their arms, ammunition, and ponies. Further north, U.S. forces began constructing forts throughout the Lakotas' hunting grounds and stepped up their efforts to harass Sitting Bull,

Gall, and the other "hostiles" until they were forced to surrender.

Gall and the other true Lakotas, meanwhile, continued to hunt. Early in October, as the Hunkpapas were moving north toward the Yellowstone, they encountered a company of troops under the command of Colonel Nelson Miles settling in for the winter at the mouth of the Tongue River. Gall was angered by the presence of these whites, who once again threatened to disrupt the buffalo hunt. On October 11, he led a party of warriors in an attack on the soldiers' supply train, shooting several of their mules, stampeding the others, and forcing the wagons to retreat. But several days later, the supply train returned, accompanied by 200 soldiers. The Lakotas, now numbering several hundred, renewed their attack, but they were held off by the soldiers' gunfire and had to satisfy themselves with burning the grass around the troops' wagons. Finally, Gall and the other war chiefs agreed to parley with the commander of the supply train, Lieutenant Colonel Elwell Otis. The Lakotas announced that they were hungry and wanted food rather than more fighting. Nonplussed, Otis reluctantly gave them some rations and moved on.

As the Lakotas continued on their way north, Miles and a company of some 400 infantrymen followed them. North of the Yellowstone near the Tongue River at a place called Cedar Creek, the soldiers approached the Indian encampment and prepared for battle. The Lakotas, realizing they were about to face another conflict, asked instead for a meeting with the troops' commander. On October 21 and 22, Gall and Sitting Bull met Nelson Miles, the officer who was to trouble them for the next several years. Dressed elegantly in a fur-trimmed coat, Miles was as young, ambitious, and arrogant as Custer. The talks soon came to a stalemate; the war chiefs, as always, wanted the troops to leave the area so they could continue hunting, whereas Miles wanted the Indians to surrender unconditionally. Finally, the two sides came to blows, and after a brief skirmish the Lakotas fled across the Yellowstone.

At this point many of the Indians—especially the Sans Arcs and the Minneconjous—were in fact ready to surrender. Winter was approaching, much of their food had been destroyed, their ponies were thin, their ammunition was running low, and the U.S. Army seemed determined to hunt them down. The Lakotas were not used to fighting in the cold; normally, winter was a time of relaxation, when they remained bundled up in their lodges, consuming the goods they had gathered the summer before. This winter was already looking bleak, and many of the Indians felt that it would be unendurable if they had to fight. Consequently, soon after the battle with Miles, the Lakotas divided, with most remaining at the Yellowstone to surrender to the soldiers while the rest traveled north toward the Missouri with Sitting Bull and Gall.

Miles was determined to pursue the resistant Sioux, and in mid-December his lieutenant, Frank Baldwin, came across them camping near the Red Water River in about two feet of snow. Baldwin's men attacked on the morning of December 18; Gall and the other warriors held them off long enough for the women, children, and elderly to escape, but the Indians were finally overpowered and forced to flee. Following military policy, Baldwin's men then confiscated or destroyed the Indians' lodges, buffalo robes, dried meat, and utensils, and slaughtered their mules and horses.

The army's offensive continued in the following months. As the Lakotas grew more destitute, they began surrendering in ever larger numbers—leaving their hunt-

ing grounds, reporting to the agencies, and giving up their horses and arms. Even Crazy Horse turned himself in to the authorities. But other bands of Sioux and Cheyenne began crossing the northern U.S. border into Canada, out of reach of the American military, and in May, Sitting Bull and Gall followed them.

By the summer of 1877, the U.S. government had essentially accomplished what it wanted. The army had driven most of the Sioux to the agencies, where, no longer hunting or warring, they would not threaten the white settlers near them. Meanwhile, government officials had persuaded agency Indians—largely through bribery and force—to sell the Black Hills. Those Sioux who remained "hostile" had abandoned their former territory and the United States altogether. Now, U.S. officials may have thought, Gall and Sitting Bull were the Canadians' problem.

Gall, Sitting Bull, and their followers had moved up Frenchman's Creek, known in Canada as the White Mud River. About 60 miles upstream from the border, they

A Lakota encampment overlooks Frenchman's Creek, near the Canadian border. Sitting Bull, Gall, and their Hunkpapa followers camped in this region in the summer of 1877, eventually moving north into Canada, where government authorities allowed them to live peacefully for several months.

camped at a place called Pinto Horse Butte. No sooner had they arrived than they had their first encounter with a new type of white officer: the Canadian North-West Mounted Police. To the Indians' amazement, a small party of red-coated officers rode casually up to them and quietly set up their own camp. Never had white men approached the Sioux so fearlessly. Indeed, the Indians' subsequent relationship with the mounted police was to be very different from any they had known with U.S. officials.

The head of this party, Major James M. Walsh, met with the Lakota chiefs and explained his country's position: the Indians had reached the land of the Great

A member of the Canadian North-West Mounted Police prepares for a day's ride.

White Mother (Queen Victoria), and she would protect them as she protected all her children who behaved themselves—and likewise would punish them as she would punish any of her children who disobeyed her laws. Specifically, this meant that the Sioux must not cause trouble in Canada and must not return to the United States to engage in warfare and then expect protection in Canada. These terms seemed simple and reasonable, and most important, they allowed the Lakotas to live as they wished, hunting buffalo on the open prairie.

For the next several months, Canada seemed the perfect refuge for the Sioux. Gall, Sitting Bull, and their followers were left to themselves, the buffalo were plentiful, U.S. soldiers no longer hounded them, and the Canadians seemed genuinely sympathetic to their ideals. Walsh even recognized that the Lakotas needed arms and ammunition for hunting, and he allowed traders to provide strictly regulated quantities of these goods. This new Canadian life was appealing—but it was not secure.

One difficulty was that Canada already had its own Indians—including such traditional Lakota enemies as the Blackfeet (different from the Blackfoot Sioux), Crees, and Bloods. For the moment, relations between the Lakotas and these tribes were peaceful, but the buffalo would not last forever, and tensions over a shrinking food source might easily ignite an intertribal war. Furthermore, the Lakotas' presence on Canadian soil could lead to diplomatic trouble for the Canadians. For example, if a Lakota warrior crossed the border in pursuit of buffalo and attacked or raided a white party while in the United States, Canada would be held accountable. Although Walsh treated the Lakotas hospitably, his nation actually wished they would return to the United States.

U.S. officials, meanwhile, did not really want Sitting Bull and Gall to come back to the United States, but they

*A Lakota warrior
addresses U.S. and
Canadian agents at Fort
Walsh in October 1877.
At this council,
General Alfred Terry
urged the Lakotas to leave
Canada and adapt to life
at the Sioux agencies;
the Indians refused.*

did not believe they could allow the Lakotas to roam free.
In October 1877, a U.S. commission led by General Terry
arrived at a Canadian post near the Lakota encampment
and tried to persuade the chiefs to go to the agencies,
which would mean surrendering their weapons, horses,
and way of life. He told the Lakotas they would "be
received in the friendly spirit in which the other Indians
who have been engaged in hostilities against the United
States and have surrendered to its military forces have
been received." Expressing the view of most of the Lakota
refugees, Sitting Bull replied that the Americans were
lying and should go back home—which they soon did.
North-West Mounted Police Commissioner James
Macleod then reminded the Indians: "You must remem-

ber that you will live by the buffalo on this side of the
line, and that the buffalo will not last forever. In a very
few years they will all be killed."

Indeed, between 1877 and 1883, the number of buffalo
grazing between the Cypress Hills and Wood Mountains—the Lakotas' new hunting grounds—diminished
rapidly. The Lakotas felt this loss keenly, for within a
year of their arrival in Canada, their population had more
than doubled. Many of the Indians who had agreed to
settle on the U.S. agencies had eventually balked at the

*Frontier traders prepare
to transport buffalo hides
after a successful hunt.
By the mid-1870s, the buffalo
population had dropped so
drastically that Sitting Bull,
Gall, and their followers had
to struggle to survive.*

restrictions placed on them there. In the early spring of 1878, after Crazy Horse was killed by agency guards, some 2,000 Oglalas left the Red Cloud and Spotted Tail agencies and fled north to join Gall and Sitting Bull. More bands followed the Oglalas, and soon the Lakotas in Canada numbered as many as 5,000.

To complicate matters, in the summer of 1878 the buffalo changed their course and moved south across the U.S. border. As the Lakotas followed them, a general panic set in among the region's settlers, who thought of Sitting Bull and Gall primarily as the men who had killed Custer. A few Lakota warriors did in fact engage in raids on Montana settlements, and these incidents were played up by journalists and politicians in the area. Montana congressman Martin MacGinnis, who hoped the government would construct a new military post in his district, wrote: "[Sitting Bull] is endeavoring to organize the Northwest Tribes, and if he succeeds he can march a force of ten thousand men, equal to any soldiers you can put in the field, and sweep every settlement before him." Miles, meanwhile, launched a volley of letters to General Sherman arguing for a campaign against the Sioux.

Throughout the following fall and winter, the Lakotas continued to move back and forth across the Canadian border, struggling to feed themselves. While they hunted in the United States, their presence caused tensions to rise among settlers; then when they returned to their Canadian hunting grounds, they began to compete more fiercely with their Indian neighbors. Finally, in the spring of 1879, when Gall, Sitting Bull, and their followers drifted south once more to hunt, Miles got permission to fight them.

Leading nearly 700 men from the Fifth Infantry and Second Cavalry, Miles tracked the Lakotas for half the summer until an advance contingent under Lieutenant

Major James Walsh (pictured), who supervised the Lakotas at their Mud River encampment, met with U.S. Army officers William Clark and Nelson Miles during their 1879 campaign against the Indians. A more tolerant government agent than most U.S. officials, Walsh defended the Indians' right to hunt and live freely in Canada.

William Clark discovered them hunting along Beaver Creek near the Milk River. Miles joined Clark and followed the Indians to the Canadian line, where he met with Walsh, who insisted that the Indians did not want to fight and had sworn to remain in Canada.

It soon became clear, however, that no matter where the Lakotas hunted, their lives would be in danger: there were simply not enough buffalo left, either in Canada or the United States, to support all the Indians who needed them. By January 1880, the Lakotas were so destitute that they were forced to eat their own horses.

Although Sitting Bull refused to acknowledge this crisis, Gall realized that his people were beginning to starve and that unless they radically changed their way of life, they would not survive. As a leader, Gall was responsible for his people; for years, he had fought for the right to hunt buffalo to feed them. But now, with the buffalo gone, he had to do whatever was necessary to ensure that his people live. Many of the Lakotas realized how dire their situation was, and by the summer of 1880, more than 1,000 had left Canada to surrender at the agencies.

In August 1880, Gall was hunting near Frenchman's Creek when his party discovered a herd of 1,200 cattle being led by several American ranchers. Gall and his hunters surrounded the herd, but before they could move in, they spotted among the ranchers an American scout and interpreter named Edward Allison, whom Gall had known for years. Allison offered the war chief and several of his companions a steak dinner, which Gall "accepted with good grace." In the discussion that followed, Allison saw a chance to gain honor by bringing Sitting Bull and the remaining Sioux refugees into the agencies. He inquired after the older chief, and Gall encouraged him to visit Sitting Bull's camp.

Soon after this meeting, Allison traveled across a high, flat plain and over a thickly forested mountain to the Lakota encampment. He was met not by Sitting Bull, but once again by Gall, who expressed interest in leaving Canada; not only was life growing painfully difficult, Gall explained, but many of the Lakotas had friends and relatives at the agencies in the United States and wished to join them. Gall promised to meet with Allison in several weeks to discuss the terms of his surrender.

By the time the two met again at the mouth of Frenchman's Creek, it was late October, and a blizzard had already announced the approach of a severe winter. This time Allison met with both Gall and Sitting Bull, but Gall explained to him that he did not want Sitting Bull to know he was trying to negotiate the tribe's surrender. Why Gall kept his intentions secret is not clear. Perhaps he hoped to gain greater power for himself by undermining Sitting Bull's authority. He may also have been convinced that his people's lives depended on their departure from what Allison called their "uncertain, hunted existence," and he knew that Sitting Bull would never yield. In any case, Gall secretly arranged for a small party to accompany Allison to Fort Buford, promising that he and a larger group would follow.

Gall and his followers—about 23 lodges—soon left Sitting Bull's camp, and on November 25, they reached Poplar River Agency, where the Poplar joins the Missouri. While the party rested there, more Lakotas joined them, so that by December, Gall's following had expanded to as many as 73 lodges. This assembly alarmed the Indian agent at Poplar River Agency, who believed that the great war chief Gall would break his promise to surrender at Fort Buford and instead incite a rebellion among the agency Indians. On December 24, Major Guido Ilges, leading several companies of soldiers, arrived to reinforce the garrison. At this point, winter was well under way, with deep snow and temperatures as low as 35 degrees below zero. Gall and his followers were camped at a bend in the Missouri River across from the agency, in thick underbrush and cottonwood trees. Ilges stationed his soldiers on a high plateau from which the Indians were visible.

Gall met with Ilges the day after the troops' arrival and told him his people would not move on to Fort Buford until spring, as the weather was too harsh for the journey. Ilges, dissatisfied with Gall's explanation, demanded that the Indians leave by January 2. Gall replied that they could not—that it was too cold. A confrontation was imminent. What Gall really intended to do is uncertain, but according to Ilges, on the night of January 1, Gall warned a trader at the agency to leave. "You people have been kind to me in the past," he said, "and I do not want to hurt you. Tomorrow we will fight and wipe out the soldiers and kill everybody at the soldier camp."

The following morning, Ilges and his soldiers attacked. Gall's people put up little resistance. According to Allison, the war chief even showed a white flag and persuaded his people to refrain from fleeing or fighting. Consequently, the assault was brief, resulting in eight casualties among the Lakotas and none among Ilges's men. Gall was with the Lakotas when they came out to lay down their weapons. According to one of the officers there, J. M. Bell, "He came riding out on his pony with his blanket wrapped around him and arms folded and looked around him as like an old Roman as any man I ever saw." The soldiers took the Indians' guns and horses, then burned down their encampment.

Thus, in the winter of 1881, nearly 20 years after Gall first fought the white men, he was finally defeated. His surrender to Ilges must have been painful, for by the time he entered this last confrontation with U.S. forces, he had already agreed to yield his entire way of life. He simply wanted a dignified and reasonable way in which to do it. To make Gall's humiliation complete, however, Ilges demanded that he walk the full four days' journey to Fort Buford, in snow and subzero temperatures, under guard.

7

A DREAM DIES

Several months after Gall and his followers arrived at Fort Buford—where, for a time, they were quartered in an abandoned warehouse—steamers arrived to ferry the surrendering Sioux to their new home, Standing Rock Agency, near the southern border of present-day North Dakota. Floating down the river, Gall passed many familiar places: Fort Berthold, where he had been attacked by Bloody Knife and U.S. troops in 1865; Killdeer Mountain, where he had fought in 1864; Fort Lincoln, which he had attacked in 1872; Fort Rice, where he had spoken eloquently but nevertheless signed the Treaty of 1868; and finally Standing Rock itself.

The land Gall returned to was very different from the country he had left four years earlier. Signs of the white civilization he had so resisted were visible everywhere: railroads crisscrossed the ground and telegraph poles dotted the landscape; houses and towns had sprung up; yellow wheat grew and white men herded cattle where buffalo had once grazed. Ten years earlier, there had been just 5,000 U.S. citizens in Dakota Territory; now, includ-

Having adapted to reservation life, Gall appears in a studio photograph wearing a bearskin coat, a feather, and a cross.

95

ing the 17,000 who were mining in the Black Hills, there were more than 130,000. In his account of Gall's life, Edward Godfrey (who fought Gall at the Little Bighorn) wrote that when the steamer reached Standing Rock Agency, the chief, in full war paint and dress, marched down the plank toward the agency. Taking one look at the establishment, however, he turned and stalked back up.

Standing Rock Agency was a clutter of buildings— offices, shops, a school, a church, and houses—lying on the western bluffs overlooking the Missouri. To the south were the barracks, warehouse, stables, and other military buildings of Fort Yates. Farther to the south and west was a flat valley, with foothills just visible in the distance. After arriving, Gall and his people set up tipis along the river, but this was to be a temporary settlement. As agency

Standing Rock agent Major James McLaughlin (center), who encouraged the Lakotas to adopt white ways, convenes with fellow agency administrators in front of his office.

Indians, they were to abandon their familiar customs and adopt "civilized" ways, which would mean living in permanent log cabins rather than in portable tipis. It would also mean exchanging their hunting equipment for farming tools, trading their suede leggings and buffalo robes for cotton or wool clothing, sending their children to school, traveling to the agency on appointed days for rations, and giving up their old religion for Christianity. The Hunkpapas' appearance, their way of life, and their way of thinking were to change as much as their land had. Overseeing this transformation was the Standing Rock agent, a short, wiry-haired, and strong-willed man around Gall's age named James McLaughlin. Married to a Dakota woman, McLaughlin was genuinely concerned about the welfare of the Hunkpapas—but he was also adamant about "civilizing" them.

Gall was 40 years old when he reached Standing Rock Agency; he was still strong and still revered by his people. Although the prospect of complying with the whites disheartened him, he must have believed that his followers depended on him, and that their interests would be best served if he pursued peaceful relations with the whites. Gall resolved to do his best to adapt to the new life.

McLaughlin recognized that Gall was a strong, principled man who had the respect of his people, and he soon befriended the war chief. Believing that the Hunkpapa leader could help him introduce "civilized" ways to the Lakotas at Standing Rock, he began to consider Gall and another warrior named John Grass the agency's head chiefs. This arrangement might have worked in everyone's favor if the two men had remained the only contenders for Lakota authority. But in 1883, Sitting Bull—who had given up his desperate life in Canada soon after Gall but had been held prisoner for nearly two years—arrived at Standing Rock, and the atmosphere at the agency shifted. Gall may have been willing to surrender his new role to the man he recognized as head chief of the Lakotas, but McLaughlin disliked Sitting Bull and would not acknowledge him. Instead, he began to pit Gall and Sitting Bull against each other, and as a result, the Hunkpapas—already weakened by their long struggle for survival and by the demoralizing act of surrender—were fragmented even further.

By the mid-1880s, the Hunkpapas had taken on many white ways. Gall, like others, had accepted Christianity, seeing in it elements of his own religion. He also supported the idea of education for Lakota children. He even accommodated the American public's interest in him, appearing at the New Orleans Exposition and speaking at a 10-year commemoration of the Battle of the Little Bighorn. Gall also learned to accept the European principle of monogamy. Sometime after his two wives had been killed at the Little Bighorn, he remarried. According to McLaughlin, in 1885, Gall fell in love with another woman and wished to marry her as well, only reluctantly abandoning the idea when McLaughlin insisted that polygamy was not "civilized."

Gall took more readily to farming, despite the difficulties posed by the land's violent freezes and parching droughts. He eventually became a "boss farmer," overseeing one of the 20 new farming districts at the agency, which grew corn, oats, wheat, potatoes, turnips, onions, beans, and other crops. By 1885, he had his own cabin and a piece of land on Oak Creek near the Missouri River.

Finally, Gall and many other Hunkpapas were living much the way government agents had always hoped. Yet the settlers around them were still not satisfied. Claiming that the Indians were not using all of the land they were allotted, throughout the early 1880s, the Hunkpapas'

Clinging to remnants of their traditional culture, an Indian family ekes out a living on a reservation allotment.

neighbors pressured the government to open up reservation land to non-Indian settlement.

The settlers' desire for Indian land was supported both by the government and by some of the philanthropists, journalists, and citizens' groups who took an interest in Indian affairs. These humanitarians believed that before the Sioux and other Native Americans could become "civilized," they needed to give up their tribal way of thinking. According to their view, each Indian family needed to have its own plot of land instead of sharing the entire reservation with the tribe, and each man needed to speak for himself in political matters rather than allowing a chief to serve as his representative. These ideas, together with pressure from settlers, led to the passage of the General Allotment Act of 1887, sponsored by Senator Henry L. Dawes. According to the Dawes Act, as it was known, each Indian family would get 160 acres, after which the remaining land would be opened for settlement by non-Indians.

Shortly thereafter, the Sioux Act, which applied the Dawes Act specifically to the Great Sioux Reservation, was introduced to Congress. The Sioux Act estimated the amount of land required by Indian families and outlined six small reservations comprising that amount of land, leaving the rest of the Great Sioux Reservation—about 10 million acres—to be opened up for settlement. To be passed, however, this act required the signatures of three-fourths of the adult males on the reservation. A commission led by Captain Richard Henry Pratt arrived at Standing Rock Agency on July 23, 1888, to persuade the Indians to sign.

All of the Lakota chiefs were opposed to the act. Meeting in council to discuss the problem, they elected four chiefs to represent the tribe. Gall was one of the four, and he gave the following speech at the meeting:

> We should listen to the whites and learn what they have to say, and then we should without foolish speaking think what we should do. Former commissions have come among us and made many promises. They did not tell us what the great father said, but talked to please the Indians' heart. In the past I have not complained of this. I believe the great father was honest, and have acted with a good heart, but unless this treaty is fair and we are told the truth, my heart will not be good.

When Pratt and the others learned that the Lakotas were intending to negotiate through their chiefs, they tried to persuade them to change their minds, arguing that each man should make his own decision. But Gall told his people, "I have been among you for many years. You know me as your chief, and you know me to be always true to you. Whom will you follow, the commission, whom you have never seen, or your chiefs, who have led you in battle and fought for you?"

Lakota children gather for a class picture outside the schoolhouse at Rosebud Agency, some 200 miles south of Standing Rock.

The talks began, and the commissioners, who had been unable to persuade the rest of the tribe to sign, tried their utmost to secure the chiefs' signatures. But Gall and the others stood firm: they would not part with more land. Finally, the commissioners decided that the Indians must sign either a black paper to accept the act or a red paper to reject it. "They come here with two papers," Gall said angrily, "and tell you we must sign one or the other, and our names will be counted. . . . This is the first time I ever knew that any man can be made to sign a paper against his will." After a month of haggling, the commission gave up, not even bothering to go to the other agencies.

That fall, Pratt suggested that the government might warm up the resistant Lakotas by bringing them to Washington. So in mid-October 1888, Gall rode his former enemy—the railway—on his first trip to the

capital. There he and the other 60 chiefs selected for the journey stayed at the Belvedere Hotel and visited the zoo and the Smithsonian. Gall was even invited to dinner at an expensive restaurant by Edward Godfrey, an army veteran who had fought at the Battle of the Little Bighorn. Reporters followed the chiefs everywhere; one journalist from the Washington Post described Gall as a "big, stout, bully fellow" and wrote that "the big Sioux mogul took to oysters in the shell like a Norfolk oysterman." Gall, who had been given some money to spend while visiting, was later asked what he bought. He replied,

> I went about your great city and saw many people. Some had fine clothes and diamonds; others were barefoot and ragged. No money to get something to eat. They are beggars, and need your help more than the Indian does. I gave them the money you gave me. All people are alike among the Indians. We feed our poor.

Gall had been forced to give up his guns, his hatchet, his ponies, and Wakan Tanka—but he had not lost the great Lakota virtue of generosity.

While in Washington, the Sioux delegates also met to discuss a new version of the Sioux Act, which offered one dollar per acre for their land. After much debate, they finally settled on $1.25 per acre. In agreeing to this, most Sioux probably believed that the price was so high that the government would not consider it, and the issue would be closed. Toward the end of October, they boarded the train and rode home.

But the Hunkpapas had underestimated the government's interest in their land. In the spring of 1889, a new Sioux Act was proposed, one that accepted the higher price demanded by the Indians. A new commission led by the Lakotas' old opponent, General Crook, traveled to the Great Sioux Reservation, reaching Standing Rock in June 1889.

Gall and John Grass (right), the head chiefs of Standing Rock Agency, pose beside a government official during their 1888 trip to Washington, D.C. At the capital, Gall, Grass, and 58 other Lakota chiefs met with legislators to discuss the Sioux Act, a measure that was to reduce the size of the Lakota reservations by more than half.

Again the Indians met in council and agreed to have the same few chiefs represent them; again those chiefs were determined to resist the proposal. But Crook's negotiating skills were more subtle than Pratt's had been. While deluging the Indians with complex terms and details of the act, he managed to speak to the chiefs separately and weaken their defenses. Meanwhile, McLaughlin met secretly with John Grass and convinced him that if he did not support the act, the consequences would be grave, because "Congress might pass the law regardless of the attitude of the Indians in the premises." This might mean that they would get no compensation at all for their land, not an unlikely possibility given the government's record in following through on promises. McLaughlin later met with the other chiefs, including Gall, and likewise pressured them to change their positions.

When the Indians and commissioners convened for a second round of negotiations, the Lakotas' attitude had changed considerably. Grass was the first of four chiefs to sign the act. A second chief followed suit. But when Gall's turn came, he suddenly refused to sign, perhaps realizing how few of his people wanted to part with more land. At this point, Sitting Bull, who had not been informed of the meeting and was adamantly against the act, arrived outside the council room with a group of followers and tried to break up the meeting. He was driven away by the Indian police. After this incident, there was a stampede to sign the papers, as people feared they would be punished if they did not sign.

On August 3, 1889, the new act passed, and more than half the Sioux reservation was sold. The Lakotas' lands, which in Gall's youth had covered large parts of what is now North and South Dakota, Nebraska, Montana, and Wyoming, could now fit into an area a third the size of South Dakota.

On ration day, hundreds of
Lakota women line up to
receive their quotas of bacon,
cornmeal, flour, coffee, and
sugar. As impoverished as the
Lakotas were, in 1890,
Congress voted to reduce
their rations by 20 percent.

The Sioux Act of 1889 deeply embittered the Lakotas.
And soon after it passed, they learned that Congress had
decided to deplete their resources even further by cutting
their rations of beef. This hardship, coupled with failed
crops and a severe winter that killed much of their
livestock, caused widespread hunger among the Sioux,
and as the Indians weakened, many of them fell victim
to influenza and whooping cough.

The Lakotas, who had been prospering only two
decades before, were now weaker and more demoralized
than they had ever imagined possible. Their life of
independence, of roaming on the open prairies or resting
in the shady Black Hills, of hunting and warring, of

believing in Wakan Tanka and Wi and the dramatic rituals that went with them had all slipped away. The Lakotas were now reduced to living in small, dark cabins and farming a tiny plot of dry ground. With illness running rampant and never enough food, they had little to look forward to.

But then, from the west, came a glimmer of hope. During the summer of 1890, the Lakotas heard of a Paiute holy man named Wovoka, who told of the coming of the Indians' messiah. Wovoka's message was simple: those who accepted his faith (a mixture of Indian spirituality

Arapaho Indians perform the Ghost Dance, a ritual introduced to the Sioux reservations in 1890. Members of the Ghost Dance movement hoped their sacred songs and dances would lead them to a life of happiness and freedom.

and Christianity) and participated in a special "Ghost Dance" ritual would be saved from their destitution and live forever in a blissful land populated by buffalo and all the Indians who had ever lived. There would be no white people, hunger, or disease in this paradise, which was destined to come in the spring of 1891.

Neither Gall nor Sitting Bull believed in Wovoka's prophecy. But so many of the Sioux did believe—and with such desperate earnestness—that Sitting Bull, as a spiritual leader of his people, felt obliged to look into the movement. He allowed Wovoka's followers to perform the sacred Ghost Dance near his home that fall. Leaving behind their cabins, the dancers set up tipis, a sweat lodge, and a prayer tree—similar to the sacred pole of the Sun Dance—and each morning they went through elaborate purification rituals before beginning the dance around the tree, wearing specially painted "ghost shirts." The participants sang and danced until, one by one, they fell to the ground exhausted.

Gall, who had become a judge on the Court of Indian Offenses in 1889, worried that the Ghost Dance movement might somehow provoke violence. The Indians who were swept up in the movement had genuine grievances, and the Ghost Dance songs, which drew inspiration from the hunt, often mentioned arrows and knives. Many reservation officials feared insurrection. By the fall of 1890, the head of Pine Ridge Agency was growing frantic. "We have no protection, are at the mercy of these crazy dancers," he telegraphed to Washington on November 12. Within days, 3,000 troops arrived at the reservations, most of them assembling at Pine Ridge. Meanwhile, Gall urged the dancers to abandon the movement and sent messages to McLaughlin asking for assistance in case a confrontation occurred.

The Ghost Dance did lead to violence, but it was not

initiated by the dancers. Rather, it was started by McLaughlin himself, who grew anxious about Sitting Bull's "troublemaking" role in the movement and ordered his arrest. Early in the morning on December 15, Lakota Indian police arrived at Sitting Bull's cabin. While attempting to arrest the old chief, however, they angered his family and the dancers camping in tipis nearby. A scuffle broke out, shots were fired, and Sitting Bull was killed.

Many historians have speculated that this was precisely what McLaughlin, angered by what he believed was Sitting Bull's obstinacy, had wanted all along. To the Indians, it must have been deeply demoralizing to learn that the old chief—the supreme leader of the Lakotas—had been killed by his own people carrying out the order of a white man.

The violence was not over, however. When the army had arrived at the reservation, many of the dancers had grown frightened and fled. A Minneconjou warrior named Big Foot and many of his followers had taken refuge in the canyons of the Dakota Bad Lands. Near Wounded Knee Creek on the night of December 28, Big Foot's band was surrounded by the Seventh Cavalry. Big Foot put out a white flag, and the following morning, he and his followers began surrendering their weapons. As the party prepared to return to the agency, however, there was a moment of confusion, and suddenly the soldiers opened fire on the Indians. Half the Sioux men were killed in the first volley, and most of the women and children fell in the shooting that followed. Those who ran were chased down and slaughtered. In the end, more than a hundred Sioux lay dead. Most of them were women and children, and almost all were unarmed. That night a blizzard raged, covering the bodies, and two days passed before anyone saw the carnage.

Years later, a Lakota holy man named Black Elk remembered the tragedy at Wounded Knee:

> I can still see the butchered women and children lying heaped and scattered along the crooked gulch as when I saw them with my eyes still young. And I can see that something else died in the bloody mud and was buried in the blizzard. A people's dream died there. It was a beautiful dream.

The Battle of Wounded Knee was the last significant violent confrontation between whites and Native Americans. That same year, the superintendent of the census, observing that white settlements now dotted the entire country, announced that "there can hardly be said to be a frontier line." In 1890, the Lakotas' dream of preserving their land and their culture against the persistent aggressions of whites lay in ashes.

Four years later, Gall's life came to a close. Some historians say his death was the result of a drug overdose; others claim it was caused by a lingering ailment related to the wounds he sustained at Fort Berthold. His internal organs may in fact have been damaged in that attack, and possibly the drug he took was meant to heal them. Whatever the cause, Gall died in December 1894 at his home near Oak Creek, about 50 miles from his birthplace. He was 54 years old.

Gall's life spanned the most controversial period in the history of the American frontier. He was born as the wagon trains first rolled west, scattering the buffalo, and he died soon after the frontier was officially declared extinguished. For 15 years, he had waged a defensive battle against the soldiers and settlers who threatened the land and culture of his people. After the Battle of the Little Bighorn, he had been forced to surrender the land, but, moving to Canada, he had still been able to preserve his people's culture, one based on independence, bravery,

and mobility. Finally, when the Sioux faced starvation, he had been forced to surrender that way of life, too.

Gall had fought each of these changes furiously, hoping that his strength and will could defeat them. But in the end, he could see no choice for the Lakotas but to yield to the world that pressed in around them. His final decision may have reflected the last of the great Lakota

A U.S. Army officer helps count the bodies of slain Lakotas after the Wounded Knee massacre of 1891. More than 200 unarmed Indians were killed in this incident, the last major conflict between whites and Indians.

virtues: wisdom. For Gall yielded only when prudence told him that he could no longer fight. As he told his people just a few years before his death, "I think it better for us to live as we are living rather than create trouble, not knowing how it will end."

CHRONOLOGY

FURTHER READING

Bernotas, Bob. *Sitting Bull.* New York: Chelsea House, 1992.

Brown, Dee. *Bury My Heart at Wounded Knee.* 1970. Reprint. New York: Washington Square Press, 1981.

Eastman, Charles A. *Indian Heroes and Great Chieftains.* Lincoln: University of Nebraska Press, 1991.

Fielder, Mildred. *Sioux Indian Leaders.* Seattle: Superior, 1975.

Josephy, Alvin M., Jr. *The Civil War in the American West.* New York: Knopf, 1991.

Lazarus, Edward. *Black Hills/White Justice: The Sioux Nation Versus the United States, 1775 to the Present.* New York: HarperCollins, 1991.

McLaughlin, James. *My Friend the Indian.* Boston: Houghton Mifflin, 1910.

Utley, Robert M. *The Lance and the Shield.* New York: Holt, 1993.

Vestal, Stanley. *Sitting Bull: Champion of the Sioux.* 1932. Reprint. Norman: University of Oklahoma Press, 1989.

Waldman, Carl. "Gall (Pizi)." In *Who Was Who in Native American History.* New York: Facts on File, 1990.

INDEX

PICTURE CREDITS

JANE SHUMATE studied classical literature and mythology at Princeton University and creative writing at Columbia University. She has also written *Sojourner Truth and the Voice of Freedom*, and *Sequoyah*, another book in the Chelsea House series NORTH AMERICAN INDIANS OF ACHIEVEMENT. Shumate lives in Philadelphia.

W. DAVID BAIRD is the Howard A. White Professor of History at Pepperdine University in Malibu, California. He holds a Ph.D. from the University of Oklahoma and was formerly on the faculty of history at the University of Arkansas, Fayetteville, and Oklahoma State University. He has served as president of both the Western History Association, a professional organization, and Phi Alpha Theta, the international honor society for students of history. Dr. Baird is also the author of *The Quapaw Indians: A History of the Downstream People* and *Peter Pitchlynn: Chief of the Choctaws* and the editor of *A Creek Warrior of the Confederacy: The Autobiography of Chief G. W. Grayson.*